Praying
in the Cellar

A VOICE FROM THE MONASTERY

Praying
in the Cellar

A Guide to Facing Your Fears
and Finding God

ANTHONY DELISI O.C.S.O.

PARACLETE PRESS
BREWSTER, MASSACHUSETTS

2005 First and Second Printing

Copyright © 2005 by Anthony L. Delisi, OCSO
ISBN 1-55725-423-0

Library of Congress Cataloging–in–Publication Data

Delisi, Anthony.
Praying in the cellar: a guide to facing your fears and finding God / by Anthony Delisi.
     p. cm. — (A voice from the monastery)
  ISBN 1-55725-423-0
  1. Meditations. 2. Delisi, Anthony. 3. Prayer—Catholic Church. I. Title. II. Series.
BX2182.3.D45 2005
248.4'82—dc22
                       2004030500

10 9 8 7 6 5 4 3 2

Published by Paraclete Press
Brewster, Massachusetts
www.paracletepress.com

*I would like to dedicate this book
to all those who have in any way brought me to this present moment.*

*I am especially indebted to
my father and mother,
my brothers and sisters,
my relatives and friends,
and to all the monks with whom I have lived during the past
fifty-seven years.*

Contents

Preface
ix

Introduction
xvii

I. Encountering God in the Cellar
1

II. Encountering God in the Darkness
35

III. Encountering God in the Light
65

IV. Encountering God in the Shade
99

Afterword
In Other Words: An Introduction to Contemplative Prayer
133

Appendix
Group Discussion Guide
145

Notes
149

Preface

In 1948, my Texan novice master and I stood near the garden in front of what we referred to as the old "Pine Board Monastery," because at that time the monks were living in a building made of pine boards cut on the property. The novice master was one of the few monks with whom I was allowed to speak. I ventured to tell him how my dad grew tomatoes back home in Pennsylvania, but my free lesson fell on deaf ears. I was told to mind my own business and be an obedient novice. I remember swallowing hard and reminding myself that I had not come to the monastery to grow tomatoes.

Now fifty-six years later I am standing in the monastic choir next to my old novice master who is now ninety-eight. I am now in charge of our tomato patch and this year's crop is abundant since I followed the directions taught to me by "Papa." The suckers were pinched off and the plants tied up.

I recall how Dad became "modern" when he bought a machine to extract the juice from the fresh tomatoes, with the pulp, skin, and tomato seeds coming out the other end, much like our digestive tract works. This eliminated the laborious process of dunking the tomatoes in scalding hot water and then skinning them. My reverie prompted me to go on the Internet, pull up a search engine, and type in "tomato machine." To my surprise, there they were. I quickly ordered one, for $39.95 plus postage, and it arrived a few days later.

We enjoyed using that machine for the first time, and soon I was making tomato sauce for our fifty monks. Mom only had to cook for the seven kids. Perhaps the sauce I am now making is not as good as Mom's, but it is good enough for monks.

The inspiration for writing *Praying in the Cellar* not only came from childhood memories, but also from reading a page from *Fire of Mercy*, by Erasmo Leiva-Merikakis, who is now a novice at our Abbey of Saint Joseph in Spencer, Massachusetts. *Fire of Mercy* is a series of meditations on the first eleven chapters of the Gospel of St. Matthew. On page 249, Erasmo writes:

> The Lord tells me to withdraw, not only into my "room" or "inner chamber," as most translations have it, but "into my storeroom," the place where I as steward

of the goods of my person, can be at the sensitive center of my own life. The storeroom is secret, hidden, because it must be safe against robbers or pilfering servants. Only I, the steward, have the key to it. Regardless of how things look in the rest of the house and garden, if provisions are dwindling in the storeroom, the life of the household cannot continue for long without being imperiled. In other words, this place is the room of truth, the space that either insures the continuing well-being of the family or threatens to wreck it. It is the inner sanctum because, determining the welfare of the home, it is its spatial heart. Its hiddenness is synonymous with its genuineness, its solitude with the solicitude the steward has invested in seeing that the table is provided for.

While reading this passage I began to think, "Where is my storeroom?" And then I remembered that when I was a child, that storeroom was the cellar. Thus, to the cellar I must go to pray!

Here in Conyers, Georgia, at Our Lady of the Holy Spirit Monastery, the monks rise at 3:45 AM each morning so that we can begin the prayer service of vigils, at 4 AM. The first part of the service, lasting about twenty minutes, concludes with a Scripture reading from the Old Testament. It is followed by a half-hour of private prayer. After reading the above passage by Erasmo, I went to the corner of the church, where I usually go to pray, and began to ponder on that early sacred place, the cellar of my childhood. My thoughts and reflections made up the original edition of *Praying in the Cellar*, published in a slightly different form in December 1997. That first edition, 2,000 copies, sold quickly at our Abbey Store, and a second printing was soon ordered.

A year later, *Praying in the Cellar* was followed by three additional booklets. The first was *Praying in the Dark Cellar*, a very difficult series of meditations to write, because I was sharing thoughts with readers that I would not have shared even with my closest friends before that. Then I wrote *Praying with the Lights On* and *Praying in the Shade*. It had been my dream that all these booklets would one day be made into a book—which is what you now hold in your hands.

Chapter one, "Encountering God in the Cellar," is a commentary on the Lord's Prayer. My prayers in this first chapter are set in italics. In chapter two, "Encountering God in the Dark," I venture into the darkest part of the cellar, namely, what for me is the banana room. In fact, there were two cellars in my childhood, since we moved when I was seven years old. The first house, which we referred to as the "old house," was in the middle of town, and the banana room where bananas were stored until they were ripe enough to sell was in that cellar. A few years ago, when I returned to my hometown of Avonmore, Pennsylvania, for the funeral of my brother, Sal, I visited that cellar, only to discover that the entrance to the banana room was walled off. I feel sure, however, that the banana room is still behind that wall.

With chapter three, "Encountering God in the Light," the lights of the cellar are finally turned on. Here I begin to reflect on the Scripture readings which come after the first nocturn (part) of vigils. Slowly my prayer becomes more contemplative. I recall my pilgrimage to France for the 900th anniversary of the founding of Citeaux, where our Cistercian Order had its beginnings. This is followed by some personal recollections of my experiences in Africa, including an encounter with death in Nigeria.

"Encountering God in the Shade," chapter four, includes the testimonies of other people who have ventured into their own cellars. One might call this experience a "healing of our memories." It is my hope that you, dear reader, will also venture into your own cellar and while there you will face your fears, exposing them fully to God, our Father. This chapter also includes some of my reflections on what it means to pray in God's light, while also desiring God's shade.

It is Jesus Himself who invites us to enter into the cellar and then, according to an older Greek version, to lock its door, descend the steps, and in the darkness let those fears surface to consciousness. What is to be done once we become aware of our fears? Bring them to the Father and silently await His healing power to conquer them.

You will find a set of questions for each chapter included at the back of the book that are intended to help make these chapters become more personal for you and to encourage you in this healing process.

The experience of entering into the cellar became an adventure for me as I recalled the days of my youth. In chapter one, for example, I remember riding on the back of a "White" truck with my cousin, Baby Joe, as we went to coal mining towns to deliver produce to various general stores. "White" was the make of the truck, such as "Ford" or "Chevrolet." After the first edition of the book was printed, I began to recall the details of that ride. I wrote the following in my journal:

At the age of nine, while riding in the back of a "White" truck with my first cousin "Baby Joe," I had a vision. In that vision, I was told what would happen to me during the rest of my life. Then I heard the words, "Put this into writing." I objected by saying: "I am not very good at writing." The voice then said, "You will improve."

In the vision I was told that someday I would become a priest, like the Benedictine priests at Saint Vincent's in Latrobe, Pennsylvania, but somewhat different. Also, in time I would travel to Africa!

That took place some sixty-seven years ago. I am not sure if the word "vision" is correct, for like St. Paul, I heard words, but I don't recall seeing anything. It seemed that the words were coming from more than one person. For years I completely forgot about this experience. It was only a few years ago that I slowly began to recall the details of that trip with "Baby Joe." It was amazing when I realized that all that had been told to me then had now come to pass.

Once we enter into the cellar and expose our fears to the Father, strange things may indeed happen. Slowly we become aware of the nearness of the God who loves us. Details of childhood events may surface that have been far from our conscious minds. But this is not something to be afraid of. It is our journey back to where we came from.

It has been eight years since I first entered and locked the door leading into the cellar of my youth and began to face the fears that had haunted me as a child. It has been some time since I last ventured into that cellar, but now whenever I enter I no longer fear, for I recall the Father of Love whom I encountered in that lonely place.

Now I face another fear. My memory is slowing down, and I have a hard time recalling simple details. My body keeps reminding me of the aging process. This is not the fear of entering the cellar, but the awareness that I must descend into the grave, into that mysterious darkness from which I will never return, and yet I have no fear, since my faith assures me that even there, in the valley of death, I will encounter the light of the eternal and living Father, who made us and loves us. In His will is our peace.

A Korean edition of this book is also being published. What are the cellars like in Korea? I do not know, but surely they must be similar to the cellar of my youth, places for storing rice and other provisions in case of need. Likewise, they must be places where children fear to enter.

Thanks to the encouragement of Jon Sweeney, associate publisher at Paraclete Press, a new edition of my *Praying in the Cellar* meditations is now being published, and the four booklets have been re-edited and made into one. I pray that as you read this new edition, my brothers and sisters, you will be blessed as you venture to enter into your own cellars and there face your fears, bringing them to the Father and encountering Him who made us and loves us.

PAX.
Anthony Delisi, O.C.S.O.

I N T R O D U C T I O N

The Gospel of St. Matthew
offers this important teaching on prayer: "'But when you
pray, go to your private room, and when you have shut
your door, pray to your Father who is in that secret place,
. . . .'" According to the original Greek, this "inner room"
or "secret place" implies a storeroom. It is a place where
one stores up provisions for a time of need. I would like to
call that place the cellar. Who would ever think of going

to the cellar to pray? Who would ever think of going to such a place to find God the Father? A cellar is usually a cool, dark place, but Jesus invites us to pray in such a place. Jesus not only tells us to enter such a place but tells us to "lock" the door.

The reflections for this book often came to me between 4:30 and 5:00 AM during my time of silent prayer in the Abbey church, when I was imagining myself in the cellar of my childhood home.

It seems to me that we make prayer more difficult than we should. We need to become like children in our approach to God. Jesus said, "'Unless you change and become like little children you will never enter the kingdom of heaven.'" It is my belief that children can teach us how to pray. We can learn to pray simply by watching them.

Children are very active by nature. They are able to use their imaginations and dream of castles in the sky while playing in a sand pile. They are full of energy, yet once they are in their mother's arms, fall quickly asleep.

This childlike approach to God is also found in the teachings of St. Thérèse of Lisieux, and her "Little Way." She herself was often called St. Thérèse of the Child Jesus. Due to her stubbornness as a child, her mother Zelie wrote: "You could put her in the cellar for a whole day and she would spend the night there rather than saying yes." Little did she know that her child, with all her faults, would someday become a saint and a Doctor of the Church.

I remember the cellar of my childhood. The cellar was the place in the house where Mom would store enough jars of tomato sauce to last us until the next harvest of tomatoes, the following summer. This was the place where the strawberry jam, elderberry jelly, and jars of peaches and blackberries were kept. The barrel of newly pressed grape juice was placed there until it became wine, and it was there that the wine was added to the wine vinegar bottle to give it a special kick. The Irish potatoes were also stored in that cellar.

This cellar of my youth had a coal room, a furnace room that was also the laundry, and the banana room. We feared this room because whenever we misbehaved, Papa would threaten to lock us children in the banana room for a time. My brother Joe was often locked in for talking back.

In the following meditations, I enter into the secret chamber, the cellar of my youth. With St. Thérèse as our guide, I invite you to join me. May you also enter into your childhood, and share your memories with God, our Father, who made us and loves us.

I

Encountering God in the Cellar

4 : 3 0   A M

I a m   a t   p r a y e r in my Abbey church. With my imagination I see myself in the cellar of my youth among the jars of tomato sauce, fruit, jams, jellies, Irish potatoes, and the moonshine barrel of new wine. I close and bolt the door, and I wait. Memories of the past come floating into my consciousness and my imagination begins to work.

What kind of a place is this? Maybe I should unlock this door and get out of here! But no, I will just stay here among these jars of tomato sauce and other preserves and see if Jesus is correct in telling me to come to this store-room to pray.

Not only am I invited to enter, I am also asked to lock the door. Why should I ever want to lock myself in the cellar with all these jars? Instead, what I am really inclined to do is scream loudly in order to get out. Okay, I'll give this thing a try, obey the words of Jesus, remain in this cellar, behind the locked door, and see what happens.

It is dark and lonely, but I am here to experience the Father. In this silence and solitude I sit and wait. With no place to go and nothing to do, I simply wait. Where do I go from here?

4 : 3 0   A M

Jesus, please don't ask me to enter into the cellar of my youth to pray.

A s   I   b e g i n   t o   p r a y   I recall other locked doors. In my little hometown we had a general store run by Porter T. Sturgeon. Part of this store had a dirt floor and was filled with outdated clothing going back to the beginning of the twentieth century. The public was not allowed into that part of the store; it was even rumored that a tree was growing there. The place was dark and dirty, with only one narrow entry and a light burning over the old cash register. About ten feet from the cash register was the potbellied stove that turned red in mid-winter, but was only able to heat the space within five feet of the glow. P. T. Sturgeon made life possible for a lot of people during the Great Depression because he sold on credit long before the days of credit cards. Behind the store, he kept a wild dog. We kids were sure that it was a wolf and were petrified as we ran past the pen. It was said that Sturgeon let the dog into his store at night. When locking up, he also tied a string from the door handle to the trigger of a shotgun aimed at the door. If anyone dared to break in at night, he was sure to be shot on the spot! I remember peeping through that front door on a Sunday and seeing the shotgun aimed at me. Those were the days when all stores closed on Sunday. I'll lock my cellar door, but I don't see the need to set up a shotgun.

4 : 3 0 A M

S i t t i n g i n t h e d a r k n e s s of this Abbey church, I recall my journey to Nigeria in 1979 which gave me the opportunity to visit my aunt and two first cousins in Sicily for the first time. I remember how my relatives would lock and then bolt the front door of their house with a large piece of timber. It would have taken an armored tank to break through!

My memory now turns to Africa and my visit in 1981 to the little village of Abidu in the mountains of the Cameroon jungles. The twenty or so houses were made of mud blocks and thatched grass roofs. Some villagers were telling me in pidgin English that they wanted to go to Nigeria to earn money. I asked, "Why go to Nigeria? This is nice here. Why do you lock your doors at night?" They answered: "To keep out the wild animals." My reply was: "In Nigeria, they lock the doors to keep out the armed robbers."

Here I am in this Abbey church and I find myself in the cellar of my youth trying to pray among these jars of tomato sauce, yet my memory takes me all over the world.

The jars of tomato sauce remind me of the times my big brother would dunk the tomatoes into boiling water and we kids would skin them. Mom would spend all day cooking down the sauce before pouring it into Ball-brand glass jars. Papa reminded us that his mother in Sicily would dry tomatoes in the sun. They would be cut in half, salted, and covered with a little olive oil to keep away the flies, then they were put in the hot Mediterranean sun to dry. Thanks to Christopher Columbus and the early discoverers of America, tomatoes were introduced into Italy. What would Italian cooking be without tomatoes?

4 : 3 0 A M

Again I am meditating in the Abbey church, and again I find myself in the cellar along with all these jars of tomato sauce. Sitting in this dark, cool room with the door locked, I wait, wanting to pray to my Father in heaven.

Memories come floating in. Are these memories of the past a gift from the Father above? These memories of the past renew fears I tried to suppress in the dark cellar of my life long ago. Fears—darkness, the Banana Room, wild dogs, facing a shotgun looking me in the eyes. All these fears I must face as I sit among these jars in the silence of this Abbey church. Yes! The ability to face the fears of the past is a grace from You, Father.

I am called to face the reality of who I am and where I have come from. Only then can I begin to pray. I am not

an African, Indian, Chinese, or Jew. Here I sit among
these jars, the son of Sicilian immigrants, born in the small
town of Avonmore, Pennsylvania, with a general store run
by P. T. Sturgeon. If I were in Africa, I would be sitting in
a yam barn made of tree branches and palm leaves with no
roof, but open to the sky. I am not in Africa, but instead I
am among these tomato jars. I sit here and wonder about
the meaning of it all. What is the meaning of life? What is
the purpose of waiting for something to happen?

Once again I find myself in the cellar among the jars,
locking myself in. This door reminds me of another door
in Rome, Italy, along the street not far from the Abbey of
San Anselmo. Tourists peep through the keyhole to get a
glimpse of the dome of Saint Peter's in the distance. If I
look through the keyhole of the door in this dark, cool
room, am I able, with faith, to see the gates of heaven and
the heavenly Father peeping down at me in this room?
Does this make sense? Why should I lock myself in this
room with the old moonshine barrel now filled with new
wine?

4 : 3 0 A M

When my brother Joe was locked
in the banana room, my oldest brother, Anthony, would
sneak down to unlock the door. Papa could not understand how Joe was able to pick that lock. When Papa
asked the other kids how Joe had gotten out, no one
would answer. I now wonder how often my brother
Anthony told the priest in that dark confessional that he
had told a lie. In those days my name was not Anthony,
but Luigene, a unique name. My baptismal record reads

"Luigi," after the saint of youth, St. Aloysius. I was the youngest of seven children: Anthony, Joseph, Francis, Salvatore, and two sisters, Catherine and Josephine. Including Mom and Dad, there were nine of us. We had to make a lot of tomato sauce to last through the winter.

I wish someone would come along to let me out of here and tell me I am wasting my time. But I know that will not happen since I have locked myself in. I intend to stay here to see if my Father in heaven really looks down into this cellar and hears my voice. Thus far, all I have been able to do is bring up the fears from my youth. Perhaps this is the first stage of prayer; the Father is giving me an insight into who I am and from whence I have come.

Perhaps instead of bringing up memories of my youth, I ought to think about the Father. In Matthew, Jesus tells me to go into this cellar and lock the door. Then "pray to your Father." Instead of waiting for something to happen, perhaps I ought to start praying. What should I say? Jesus then goes on to tell me not to pray like the Gentiles who use a lot of words. He says, "You should pray like this: 'Our Father . . .'" Okay, here goes—*"My Father."* No! not *"My Father,"* but *"Our Father."* Gee, here I am locked in by myself, but I am not praying by myself! It is not *my* but *our.* I am not praying by myself, but with others. Here I am praying for Papa and Mama, and my brothers and sisters. I am speaking on their behalf and calling God "Our Father." I am praying on behalf of all my buddies and playmates in the street. I am praying for Porter Sturgeon. I am praying on behalf of everyone I have ever encountered during my life, my high school and college friends, Peewee, Flycatcher, Lanzi, Gene Kerr, my fellow monks, the monks and nuns in Nigeria and the Cameroon. On behalf of them all, and all humankind, I go to God "Our Father"—here among these jars of tomato sauce.

4 : 3 0   A M

O n c e   a g a i n   in this Abbey church, I find myself in the canning cellar behind the locked door pondering the word "our." This is similar to the first time I ventured into the Heart of Jesus only to discover that I was not alone. There were hundreds, thousands, and millions of others with me in that Heart. They spoke to me by their silence and example. This morning in this dark, cool cellar, I find them with me as I pray *"Our Father."* Not only do I pray on their behalf, but I especially pray in the Name of Jesus who taught me to call God "Our Father." Jesus is now teaching me how to pray in this cellar; the cellar that symbolizes the very hidden chambers of my being.

Jesus! Who is Jesus? He is by nature the Son of the eternal Father; He shares His Sonship with me so that I dare call God "Our Father." Jesus! Who is Jesus to me? I would like to say Jesus is to me what He is to Mother Teresa. Twice I have been in her presence and spoken with her. Twice I have experienced the power of her personality as she recognized Jesus within me. To her, Jesus is truly "the Word made flesh."

Jesus is the bread of life.

Jesus is the hungry .... to be fed.

Jesus is the thirsty .... to be satiated.

Jesus is the naked .... to be clothed.

Jesus is the sick, the lonely, the unwanted, the leper, the beggar, the drunkard, the little one, the blind, the dumb, the crippled, the prisoner, the old.

Her litany goes on and on. She saw Jesus in everyone that came into her life as she saw Jesus in me.

In this cellar, I pray with Jesus for all, as we pray together: *OUR FATHER.*

5 : 0 0 A M

Returning to my place in the monastic choir with my fellow monks, we pray Psalm 77. This psalm expresses where I have been during my half-hour of meditation: "I thought of the olden days, years long past came back to me. I spent all night meditating in my heart. . . ."

Our next psalm, 139, speaks of You, my God and Father. "If I climb the heavens, you are there; if I lie in Sheol, you are there too." Or in my experience—*"if I go down into the wine cellar, You are even there. Our Father in heaven is in this cellar with me."* Jesus invites me to go to such a place to pray to our Father. *"Father, why are You present in a special way in this cellar? Is it because this place symbolizes the very depth of my being, and how You, my God, provide for all of our needs? We call You Father. In a very special way You are a Father for all that was and is and is to come. Abba, Pater, Father!"*

4 : 3 0 A M

To the sound of rain falling on the Abbey church, I go to my corner to pray in the silence of the night. I begin with the Divine Mercy Chaplet, saying over and over again: "Have mercy on us and on the whole world." Just as with the "Our Father," I do not pray alone, but in union with Jesus and all humankind. *In the silence of this night I pray with and for all humankind to You, O God, to have mercy on us.*

With my imagination, I find myself again among the jars of tomato sauce. "Here I recall my earthly father, Your gift to me as an external sign of Your ever eternal love as a Father."

Dad was born in Termini Imerese, Sicily, in 1885 of very poor parents. He was the first born of my grandmother, who was an orphan. Papa would remind us that the only parts of a chicken they could afford to buy were the head, neck, and feet. I remember on special occasions Papa ordered a chicken from a local farmer. Mama would go through the ritual of wringing its neck and hanging it feet up until it stopped moving its wings. This ritual of death did not impress me. It didn't make sense to see that chicken fighting for life only then to die. But this was my first initiation into death. Mama would then dunk the chicken into boiling water. We kids would have to pluck it until it was naked.

My second experience with death came while I was in the second grade, when Granddad was kidnapped by the Mafia. He then had a stroke and died in the hospital. I stood by his coffin and touched his cold, hard, motionless hands. We called him "Babi" (short for "Babianni"). This word probably originated from the Arabic word for father: "Baba" plus "annus" equals "father of many years" or grandfather. He was a "capo" and head of the Sicilians in our area of Pennsylvania. (This is not the place to go into Granddad's history).

4 : 3 0   A M

F r o m   t h i s   A b b e y   c h u r c h   I again descend into the cellar of my youth, to meditate among the jars of tomato sauce. My memory is much like this cellar, where I store away the events of each passing day until once again they surface. It reminds me where I have come from, who I am, and where I am going. *Yes, I am going to You, our Father, who knows me. You know my past and where I have been. You know all about my earthly father and my Babianni and all those who preceded me and brought me into the darkness of this Abbey church. You are a God of history and Your book, the Bible, is filled with memories of the past. In the same way, I dip into my own memories to help me pray to You in this present moment.*

Yesterday I was meditating on death, the death of a chicken, the death of Babi, and now I recall a day in 1986 when I was a chaplain to the nuns of Abakaliki, Nigeria. On that day a strange sound came from the village. Peter and Augustine, our workmen, told me it was wailing, indicating that someone had just died.

I also recall Good Friday, 1982, in the Cameroon. We were celebrating the Liturgy and had finished reading the Gospel on the death of Jesus. A native began beating on a drum, made from a hollowed-out log, notifying those living in the jungle that the son of the king had just died. The sound of the drum went on and on and touched the very center of my being. Jesus died for these people in the jungles of the Cameroon.

In Nigeria it was not the hollowed-out log, but the loud wailing of the village women that indicated that someone had just died. The deceased was a man about thirty years old leaving behind a wife and a young son. That evening I was invited to the funeral of Clement. Just before sunset I arrived at his home made of mud blocks and a grass roof. His body was lying under a tree and covered with a palm mat to keep off the flies. They uncovered the corpse. I looked down and saw his right arm covered with some chicken feathers, and drenched with chicken blood. I did not know the significance of this ritual.

Later, Peter and Augustine explained the ritual of the pagan death. After death, one of the elders kills a chicken over the corpse and lets the blood flow onto the right arm. The bird is flung as far as possible into the bush. One of the villagers claims the dead chicken and in exchange gives yams to the family of the deceased. Yams to the Nigerians are like bread to the European, or rice to the Asian.

Father, is this a continuum of the rituals of the Old Testament? The Ibo people claim to be the Jews of Africa. Death, blood, and food make up the ritual given to us by You, our Father. At sunset the men took Clement's body and ran with it toward his yam patch. There they had prepared a round hole within which was a rectangular grave where the corpse was placed. The women wailed. The elders of the village began pouring the native moonshine called *kiki* into the grave. The favorite drink of the deceased determined the kind of drink poured into the grave. It could be wine, beer, *kiki*, or even Coca-Cola. The grave was covered with logs and palm branches, and men started throwing in the dirt. Here he was, planted among his yams. Darkness set in and it was night.

4 : 3 0 A M

In this early morning, I call upon You, Father, to acclaim Your name of father as holy. To be able to know You by name means that You have made known to me Your name through Your only Son, Jesus Christ. You are holy, since You are also "Our Father."

As Your son, I enter into this cellar to be among these jars of tomato sauce.

M o m r e a l l y k n e w h o w t o c o o k with tomato sauce; she added fresh basil, garlic, pepper, and other herbs. Chicken tasted great when it was cooked in this sauce. My brothers preferred the drumsticks, but I liked the white meat. Papa always ate the head, neck, and feet. By nature, I must be a vegetarian, since the only meat that I like is that white meat from those chickens. Oh, I forgot about the meatballs cooked in this sauce. Mom knew how to mix the ground beef with Italian bread crumbs, eggs, and grated cheese that we kids had ground with the hand grinder. She added her spices, fried the balls of meat in olive oil, and put them into the sauce. When Mom took veal and dipped it into bread crumbs, my dislike of meat vanished. On Sundays Dad would grill steaks over the coals burning in the furnace in this cellar; then Mom would cover them with olive oil, rub in the garlic, and sprinkle on oregano. Generally I didn't like fat either, but that fat, dripping onto the coals while being grilled, had a unique aroma. *Father, it reminds me of sacrifices given to You by the people of Israel in times of old. Will they once again offer animals in a newly constructed temple in Jerusalem, or will they join us in offering to You Your beloved Son, Jesus Christ? Will your people honor your name as revealed to us through your only Son Jesus? St. Paul tells us that they will* (Romans 11).

4 : 3 0   A M

O n c e   a g a i n   I find myself with the jars of
sasa—the Sicilian word for tomato sauce, which rhymes
with Papa and Mama. That Sicilian word is similar to the
word for sausage: *sazitsa*. Mama knew how to take the
pork and blend it with fennel seeds and a bit of hot pepper to make a mild Italian sausage. She would take hog
guts, preserved in salt, wash and place them on the end of
a special wide-mouthed funnel. Papa would begin to stuff
the casing. It took extra strength to keep that pork going
into the funnel. My job was to take a needle and punch
holes into the air pockets seen in the sausage being
formed. Mama then twisted the sausage to form the links
and hung them out to dry.

Mama also often cooked the *sazitsa* in tomato sauce.
At times, Papa broiled the sausage over the coals in
the furnace of this cellar. The sausage was then covered with lemon juice and ah, what a taste! Our Jewish
neighbors next door could not share in this feast, but on
Passover they shared with us their matzos. *When will*
that day come when Your people will accept Your Son, Jesus,
and become part of Your Kingdom? "Thy Kingdom come."
When will peace come between the Israelites and the
Palestinians? When will the day come when Your kingdom
will be established throughout the earth?

4 : 3 0   A M

Our Father, You are in this Abbey church and You are with me
as I descend into the cellar of my childhood memories. Your

kingdom must first come into my heart and into every heart before You will establish it upon this earth.

The green banana bunches hanging in this banana cellar bring me into contact with the ends of the earth. Each bunch of bananas has a history all its own. Who picked it? How did it get to Pittsburgh, and from there to the railroad siding in Saltsburg near where my uncles lived?

My uncles (all of them named Joseph) would get their sons, and Papa would get my older brothers to help unload the bananas. Then they were distributed into the banana cellars of different homes. We were afraid that in one of those bunches a poisonous spider from the tropics might be hiding. The dark, green bunches of bananas hung in the dark room, in the heat and high humidity. Slowly, the bunches began to ripen. Each bunch was placed into a round banana basket, which was about five feet high and had a burlap pocket set into the top. At times my first cousin Baby Joe and I would watch those baskets being loaded onto the old "White" truck along with other fruits and vegetables. They were delivered to the general stores in the different coal mining towns: Slickville, Coal Run, Tin Town, Salina. Baby Joe and I would ride behind with the produce and, at times, hide under the banana blankets used to keep the fruit safe from windburn.

You, Father, must have looked down upon us as we traveled with those bunches of bananas. The bunches were hung in the general stores. Smaller bunches were cut from the large bunch with a specially shaped "banana knife."

4 : 3 0   A M

"Thy Kingdom come." Jesus, be King of my heart, be King of all hearts. May Your Kingdom be established in all the lands of the world, including the depths of this cellar.

B a n a n a s are a unique fruit. They are shipped all over the world; but once they begin to ripen, they last only a few days. Papa would at times be called "Joe Banan" by the men in the streets.

The bananas now hanging in this cellar remind me of Nigeria. At times I was assigned to drive one of the nuns to the market—Sister Appolonia, Sister Nnaemeka, Sister Chineottito, or Sister Ife Christe. Taxis filled with people would come rolling in from the Cameroon border. Piled high atop the roofs were bunches of bananas. They were unloaded at the taxi park and then the natives would start bartering. Since I was *onyeocha*, "white man," the price usually was higher for me. The sisters were better at bartering, but in time my reputation grew, and I became known as a white Ibo.

At other times, Sylvester, a small old man, would help us locate the best buys. One day he confided to me that he had no food or money for his family. *Jesus, You tell us that "our almsgiving must be in secret."* The day came when we were notified that Sylvester had died. *He was taken into Your Kingdom. May he be blessed for the days he helped us buy bananas.*

Here in Georgia, I once had the job of buying food for the community. The bananas now came in smaller bunches packed in large boxes rather than in those large bunches.

I now recall the days when almost every household had a bowl of artificial wax fruit on the table. In our house the wax bananas were small and reddish. It was only later in Nigeria that I again saw such bananas. They were supposed to be good for pregnant women. There were plenty of pregnant women in Nigeria. *May Your Kingdom come to all the kingdoms of this earth.*

4 : 3 0   A M

On this Feast of St. Thérèse of Lisieux (October 1), I come to the corner of the Abbey church to ponder the words of that prayer Your Son has given us to pray. We pray to You, Father, that Your will be done. But how can we do Your will unless You first tell us what Your will is for us? You have spoken through Your book, the Bible, through Your Son, Jesus, and through Your gift of the Holy Spirit. Your will is that I descend into the cellar of my childhood, shut and lock the door, and call out to You as "Our Father."

Papa was an external sign of who You are to me.

E a c h   s p r i n g   Papa would go out to the lot behind the house across the alley, and turn over the soil, shovel by shovel. Tomato seeds were planted in a flat box and placed near the furnace in this cellar until they sprouted. Daily he took the flat out into the sunshine, and at night returned it near the furnace. By the time summer vacation arrived, the tomatoes were in the ground. He planted them deep so that only half the plant showed above the ground.

When I got big enough, I was assigned to hoe the weeds, but this took time away from the swimming hole. The creek across the Kiskiminitis River was dammed with burlap sacks filled with sand. We boys would swim as naked as we were born. When the plants started to grow, Papa would stake them up, pull off the wild lower suckers, and tie them up with strips of old rags which Mama salvaged from clothing too old to patch. The fifty-five-gallon drum under the downspout of the gutter on the barn saved rain water and also contained a sack of manure. This "manure tea" gave the plants that extra something to help them grow.

4 : 3 0   A M

Feast of the Guardian Angels (October 2)

The angels do Your will in heaven, and they bring Your will to this earth. They watch over and guide us. My angel is at my side as I enter in and lock this door. Alone and with my angel, I praise You, "Our Father, who art in heaven . . ." and in this cellar, this cellar of my heart, this cellar of my memory, this cellar of the center of my being, where You are a hidden God of love.

E a r t h . What does this word mean in the Greek of the New Testament? It means the arable land, the ground, the place where seeds will grow. *It is from this arable ground that Adam was made, and it is here that You want Your will to be done.* Earth, dirt, soil, dust, Georgia red clay—all of these are related.

Red clay reminds me of my entry into this monastery more than a half-century ago in 1948. The field in front of the old monastery was planted with tomatoes. The plants were growing wild and laying on the ground. Suckers were sprouting all over the place. Papa would never have grown tomatoes in such conditions. He would have hoed the plants, tied them up with pieces of old rags, pulled off the suckers, and loved the plants until they bore their marvelous fruit.

As I mentioned at the beginning of this book, one day I ventured to tell my novice master how Dad grew tomatoes. But you will remember that my free lesson fell on deaf ears. I was told to mind my own business and be an obedient novice. *I had to swallow hard and remind myself that I did not come to the monastery to grow tomatoes, but to do Your will, Father.*

That field of wild tomatoes blossomed, forming tomatoes which began to rot as soon as they touched the ground. We novices were sent to pick the few tomatoes that were small and turning ripe. Even after they were cooked down they tasted horrible in comparison with the sauce that Mama made. Papa would never have done it that way. He would have picked the tomatoes when they were almost ripe, placed them in the shade inside the garage, and waited until they had completely ripened. Only then were they cooked down to make the tomato sauce that is in this cellar with me. *I had to keep reminding myself I didn't come to the monastery to grow tomatoes, but to do Your will, O God.*

Twenty years later, I was given responsibility for the old chicken houses which were converted into greenhouses for growing tomatoes. Then, I began growing thousands of tomato plants. When they were about eight to ten inches tall we sold them. One year I had many flats of tomato plants that grew about 3/4 of an inch tall and then died. What was wrong? Calling in the experts of the state, we found that the soil lacked magnesium, a simple trace element. A pinch of Epsom salts was all that was needed.

4 : 3 0   A M

If the Greek word for "earth" means "arable soil," then perhaps every seed planted in that soil is doing Your will, Father. You are also the Father of every seed planted in the earth, giving it the power to grow, produce fruit, and then to be stored away like these jars of tomato sauce. Every vine planted in the soil, if properly pruned and cared for, produces the grapes that in turn are crushed to make the juice now turning into wine in this moonshine barrel.

This reminds me of the joke about the moonshiner that was caught making whiskey. He was taken before the judge and asked his name. "My name is Joshua," he said. The judge then asked, "Are you the Joshua that made the sun stand still?" "No sir, I'm the Joshua that made the moonshine still."

Every grain of wheat planted in the earth does Your will, Father, and grows according to the soil it is planted in and the weather conditions.

When harvested, each grain is crushed, flour made, and then shipped to the railroad siding in Saltsburg. Dad, my older brothers, my uncles named Joseph and their sons, unloaded the boxcar and stored the flour in the Saltsburg warehouse. One day while unloading the flour, it began to rain and some of the sacks got wet. What was to be done? Dad decided to approach P. T. Sturgeon and tell him about the wet bags. The flour inside was still good and so Dad sold it to Sturgeon at cost. The next time Sturgeon saw Dad he asked, "When are you going to get more of that flour at a special price?"

Every so often when we ran out of flour at home, Papa would bring in a hundred-pound bag and put it into the large tin container near the furnace to keep it dry. The empty sack was used to make tea towels.

Mama had her ritual of things to do each week. Monday, for instance, was always wash day. She sorted the clothes according to color. We had a modern spinner on our washing machine, while most people in town had to turn their wringers by hand. One of my bigger brothers hung a clothesline from the barn, around the tree, and back to the garage. First Mom hung out the sheets, then the towels, shirts, long underwear, and last of all, the work clothing. She used long tree branches to hold up the clothesline.

Tuesday was devoted to ironing, Wednesday to sewing, and Thursday to baking. Mama would come into this cellar, measure out the flour, and put it into a large pan. First she made the sign of the cross on herself, and then traced a large cross on the flour. Mama told me her mother used to do this, as did her grandmother. The warm water, yeast, shortening, and salt were then added to the flour. Then she would begin to mix and punch down the dough. The batch was covered with an old warm coat and left to rise.

Mama would punch down the dough two times according to Sicilian tradition, letting it rise, and then she would form the loaves. There is nothing like freshly baked bread with butter or some strawberry jam or elderberry jelly from this cellar! *"Give us this day our daily bread . . . and jam."*

4 : 3 0 A M

Feast of Saint Francis of Assisi (October 4) who espoused Lady Poverty

I n   t h e   c o r n e r of this Abbey church my thoughts turn to Sicily as I ponder the words *"give us this day our daily bread."* In Sicily it is the custom to always dress the table with a cloth. The loaves of bread are placed in the center along with the wine bottle. The bread is broken by hand and eaten as the companion to other foods. *Cum panis*, which means "companion," to eat bread together. Bread is the companion to other foods. If a family is very poor, the meal may consist of olives and cheese eaten with bread.

On my return trip from Africa I was privileged to also visit the Holy Land. There, my meals often resembled the meals in Sicily. In my cousins' home in Sicily, no one seemed concerned if a piece of bread was not finished and another fresh piece broken from the loaf. After the meal, the dishes were always cleared away and particles of bread saved for making bread crumbs.

Mama used to keep this bread in the drawer of the oven where the heat would help dry it out. It was left to us kids to make bread crumbs with the hand grinder. Before the time of the grinder, crumbs were made with a rolling pin. The tablecloth was always shaken outdoors to give the birds their share of the crumbs. In winter one could see the tracks of the birds in the snow as evidence of their feast. Mama had a special way of turning ordinary bread crumbs into Italian bread crumbs: dried parsley, oregano, basil, salt and pepper, and a handful of grated cheese. At times this mixture was fried in olive oil, at other times it was not, depending on its intended use. Whenever Mama ran out of bread crumbs, she would send me to P. T. Sturgeon's to buy a loaf of day-old bread sold for a nickel. Normally bread sold for a dime.

What would Italian cooking be without bread crumbs? They just seem to add something special to foods like eggplant, cauliflower, and stuffed artichokes. Also, small pieces of meat were sometimes cut to about 1/16 of an inch thick, rolled in bread crumbs, and broiled over the coals of the furnace in the cellar. These were called *brushalatini*. My memory fails me as I try to recall the Sicilian word for bread crumbs. It will probably come to me during vespers (evening prayer).

Little wonder that You, Father, through Your Holy Spirit inspired Jesus to tell the disciples to collect "the scraps remaining, twelve baskets full." Mary must have cooked with bread crumbs.

4 : 3 0 A M

Here I meditate before You, Jesus, the Living Bread come down from heaven. I ponder on the prayer You give to us whereby we call God, Your Father. I reflect on the words "give us this day our daily bread."

In the early church, St. Hippolytus of Rome, St. Chrysostom, and other church fathers wrote of the faithful taking the eucharistic bread to their homes to be eaten before any other food was consumed. This special bread was kept in a safe place, for the Body of the Lord must always be treated with the utmost respect. *In fulfillment of Your word, each Christian family partook of this special bread, the Eucharist, and thus fulfilled Your prayer: "Give us this day our daily bread."* All of the early church fathers spoke of this daily bread as the Eucharist.

Here in this cellar, You give me all I need for Eucharist. The large tin with flour, water, the hot coals in the furnace, and the new wine. I can make unleavened bread by taking the pizzelle iron hanging in the corner, wax the inner surface with the wax from a jam or jelly jar so the dough doesn't stick, mix flour and water, roll out the small dough balls, let them dry for a while, and then place them one by one inside the iron in order to bake them over the hot coals.

Over there is the new wine. Little did I realize as a child in this cellar that someday, as a priest, I would be taking the elements of bread and wine in order to pray: "This is My Body. This is My Blood," and share them with others.

Jesus becomes present with me in this cellar among the jars of tomato sauce. *Behind this locked door together we pray to You, Father, that prayer that is said at every Eucharistic celebration: "Our Father . . ."*

Papa and Mama received the special bread of the Eucharist as often as was permitted. In our mission church of St. Ambrose, Communion was permitted every other Sunday at the 8:30 AM service. At the 10:00 AM service, Communion was not given.

When I was ten years old, my sister, Catherine, entered the convent, and if I remember correctly, it was at that time that Papa, Mama, and my sister Josephine began to go to daily Mass and receive the Eucharist.

Jesus, it is You who gave us the strength to live each day through the power of Your Eucharistic presence. You wish to live within the members of Your mystical body. You wish to look upon the work of Your creation through our eyes. With St. Paul we may cry out: "I live now not with my own life but with the life of Christ who lives in me," through the power of this, our Daily Bread.

4 : 3 0 A M

Before You, Jesus, I ponder "our daily bread." It is You, Father, who give us the food of Your Son, Jesus Christ.

I n   o u r   h o u s e h o l d , bread was never served with pasta. They are not companion foods. They are like children coming from the parent of wheat. It is true that in other parts of Italy, garlic bread and pasta go together, but not in Sicily. The twenty-pound box of spaghetti was kept near the flour in this cellar.

What would Italian cooking be without pasta, bread, bread crumbs, and tomato sauce? But, there is one day each year when neither bread nor pasta are eaten—St. Lucy's Day, December 13—once considered the shortest day of the year. On that special day, we did not eat anything made from flour, since St. Lucy was martyred at a flour mill. We were, however, permitted to eat whole grain wheat cooked like rice called *cocha*, since it did not need a mill for its preparation.

A story is told in my family of Uncle Joe DeMaria, who did not observe this custom. Once, when a carload of flour arrived on St. Lucy's day, he went inside a boxcar to see if everything had been unloaded properly. Someone came along and slammed the door, and he was locked in that dark boxcar. In his fear, he prayed to St. Lucy, the saint of light, and asked to be delivered. He pounded and pounded on the door, but no one heard him. After a while, Uncle

Joe promised never again to eat bread on St. Lucy's day if he was freed. He kept pounding the door until at last it slowly opened. Finally, standing there before him was an African-American man who had heard his call.

Like my Uncle Joe, I am locked in this dark cellar, facing my memories and my fears. I cannot see, but I pray to St. Lucy for light.

I recall my visit to the Abbey of Tre Fontani in Rome and the large variety of pasta they had stored in the kitchen closet: pasta of every shape, size, and color, each with a taste all its own. There was a range of pasta from rigatoni, which we called stove pipes, right down to angel hair.

Mama used to mix all kinds of things with pasta: beans such as fava, peas, chickpeas, lima beans, lentils. With spaghetti she would add spinach, squash, or dried chestnuts, and at times just plain olive oil and garlic. During Lent we used fried bread crumbs instead of cheese on the pasta. *Thank You, Father, for giving us our daily pasta or bread, except on St. Lucy's Day.*

4 : 3 0   A M

"Our Father," we have just finished praying Psalm 44. This psalm says that You know the secrets of our hearts. If You know the secrets of our hearts, then You must be within our hearts, within our conscience, within the very center of our being—just as You are now with me as I am locked behind this door with these jars of tomato sauce and bottles of wine.

You are present in our hearts. We are not alone. We are here and You are with us. Adam, my father, and Eve, my mother, thought they were alone in the Garden when they took the forbidden fruit of the tree. You were there hidden within their hearts, but they thought they were alone. Nothing is hidden from You since You know the secrets of our hearts. Jesus, Your Son, tells us in Matthew that You see "'all that is done in secret.'" You saw Adam and Eve when they thought they were alone. You are a hidden God. To sin is to be alone, hidden from You. To sin is to say "no" to Your invitation of love. You alone know the true nature of sin while we call out to You: "Forgive us, Father. Forgive our debts, our sins, our faults, our shortcomings."

We sometimes do not recognize You hidden in the secret chamber of our hearts. Have mercy on us. Have mercy on us and on the whole world. You forgive us, so we ought to forgive one another.

I forgive my brother Joe, who thought it was funny when he threatened to drop me out the window. In this cellar I am safe from him, since the windows are high and at ground level. Here I am safe from Joe. "I forgive you, Joe. Please forgive me."

For the unknown parents of my orphaned grandmother, I ask forgiveness. For my father who ran away from his father to go to Michigan to become a servant boy to the Armour-Swift family, I ask forgiveness. For the gang in Oak Park, Illinois, involved in a shoot-out that forced my Dad to take flight to Pittsburgh, I ask forgiveness. For the men of the Mafia who kidnapped Babianni, I ask forgiveness. *You are hidden in my heart and know all my sins, and for them I ask for Your pardon. Forgive me, Lord!*

For all our secret sins that we have tried to hide from You and from Your love, we ask forgiveness.

We cry out to Mary, our Mother, to pray for us sinners locked behind this door with the bottles and jars. We ask you to plead for us with Your Son, now and at the hour of our death. Amen.

4 : 3 0   A M

"Our Father," as long as I remain behind this locked door in this cellar, as long as I can face the fears of my childhood and my youth, as long as Jesus, Your Son, the living bread from heaven is with me, I will not fear. I will not be led into temptation, for I am secure behind this locked door; I have locked myself in with Jesus.

J e s u s   p a s s e s   through the locked door and stands in our midst and says: "Peace I bequeath to you, my own peace I give to you, a peace the world cannot give, this is my gift to you."

Here I wait with dreams of the future. There are bottles of wine dated to the years of my brothers' and sisters' births. A Sicilian custom is to set aside bottles of wine from the year a child is born to be used on very special occasions during the child's lifetime, like a wedding, or the birth of a child. Since I was born during the Great Depression and prohibition times, no bottles were set aside for me. In spirit, I take some of the bottles of the new wine set aside now, to remember this day and hour and to dream of that future day when anew with Jesus, we will drink of the fruit of the vine for the great wedding of the Lamb, Jesus. *Now I can use this wine to fill this cup, to drink Your blood, and become one with You, Jesus. However great the temptations from the evil one, I will not fear, for You, Father, have invited us to pray for deliverance. "Our Father," You will deliver us. To You be given the honor and praise through Jesus, Your Son, in the Holy Spirit, forever and ever. Amen.*

I recall Brother Joseph of Awhum, Nigeria. I do not remember his Ibo name. But once I asked him how he spent the time of prayer in the darkness of the early hours in the monastery church of Mount Calvary. His answer was very simple: "I pray the 'Our Father.'"

"Then what do you do?" I asked.

"I simply pray the 'Our Father.' I have done this for two years and have yet to finish before the time of prayer is over," he replied.

Together with him, I pray, we pray, "Our Father, who art in heaven . . ." and in this cellar with the tomato sauce, preserves, and wine. You are with us, and we fear no evil. To You be praise and honor and glory forever and ever. Amen.

4 : 3 0   A M

Your will for me today, Father, is to cook for the monks. What will You provide for me to cook? What will I find in the walk-in cooler? Will it be asparagus?

M y   b r o t h e r   A n t h o n y used to grow asparagus outside the window near the coal room. In early spring, the asparagus would peep through the earth. Today it is shipped from Chile and Peru. Will my Baptist brother and friend, the Rev. Ken Board, come along to give me a helping hand? He will be able to cut off the tough ends, wash the asparagus, and put them into the steamer. They will steam just long enough to make them tender. I'll pour over them some olive oil imported from Italy.

Papa bought the cheapest olive oil from the third pressing. Today, olive oil is advertised as "virgin" or "extra virgin." It could even be widowed, but as long as it is olive oil, it is good enough for me. I'll sprinkle the asparagus with salt, garlic salt, pepper, and a little bit of grated cheese from the five-pound bag. No longer do I have to grind it with the hand grinder. That was hard work! I might fry some of the bread crumbs that Father Eduardo gathers from the bread slicer at the bakery and add salt, fresh parsley, garlic salt, pepper, and a bit of grated cheese. This will make a good topping for the asparagus. I know that Father Clarence likes mayonnaise with his asparagus, but that is not the way Mama would do it, and so neither will I. I am not sure if this is exactly the way Mama prepared it, but it ought to be good enough for the monks.

I'm sure glad that we eat vegetarian at the monastery most of the time. Why would anyone want to kill a cow just for food? The tomato sauce we use is store-bought and isn't as good as Mama used to make. Meatballs would add the finishing touch to the sauce, but it is easier for me that we are vegetarian. Even to this sauce from the can, things have to be added. Then I add Vidalia onions— grown near us in Georgia—to the olive oil in the frying pan, as well as parsley, garlic salt, oregano, basil, and mushrooms. All this is added to the sauce. I don't like the bitterness of green bell peppers, but someone recently told me how to add a fresh carrot to the sauce to remove this bitterness.

What kind of pasta should be cooked? There is not much variety: elbow macaroni, spaghetti, ziti, or egg noodles. The freezer holds frozen ravioli and tortellini. I could make a salad from lettuce from the market, but the tomatoes from the market just don't taste like the ones Dad grew. This summer, Mike, the cook at the monastery, grew some tomatoes and they were very good. I'll make mushroom soup from fresh mushrooms. Papa knew where to find mushrooms in the woods, but I didn't inherit his gift of finding edible mushrooms. Will Ruth, a friend of the monastery who is in charge of our food bank, bring some cakes or pumpkin pies? I hope so.

Father, You provide for all our needs and give to us our daily bread. For the monks that don't like my cooking, there is "Monastery Bread." Too bad that I cannot give them Gethsemani cheese from our monastery in Kentucky, or the Gouda cheese made by the nuns of Our Lady of the Angels Monastery in Virginia to go along with "Monastery Bread." There are also the jams and jellies made by the monks of Spencer Abbey in Massachusetts. They are all good, but not as good as the strawberry jam and elderberry jelly of my youth.

Thank You, Father, for providing for our daily needs. Thank You for our Daily Bread, the Eucharist, Jesus, Your Son, our Lord. Amen.

4:30 AM

"Our Father who art in heaven," You have made all that was and is and is to come. You made and make the galaxies. You are the author of it all. From the silence of Your triune Being came the "big bang" that began it all. It is You who have brought me into being to see the work of Your hand. You are now with me as I go into the memories of my childhood. I ponder and pray among these jars of tomato sauce, preserves, Irish potatoes, and new wine.

Indeed, Your name is holy. As "Our Father," You made and make all that was, and is, and is to come. You are the Father who gives to seeds the power to grow and provides for our needs both in summer and winter. You gave to Papa and Mama the know-how to set aside food for the coming days of need; and we now store these provisions in this cellar. In the cellar of my memory, I have stored away the days of my childhood and youth, that I might now remember them in prayer, to give praise to You.

When will Your Kingdom come and the Kingdom of Your Son? It will come when Your will is done in my heart and in the heart of every man, woman, and child. Your will is that I descend into the secret chamber of my being to find You in the chambers of my heart where You are hidden. You know who I am and where I have been, since You made me and are a hidden God, hidden in the very center of my being.

Your Son tells me it is Your will that I descend into this cellar to be alone with You, to expose to You my fears, to trust in You, then to rest in Your arms for You are "Our Father." This is what it means to do Your will. Here I pray, we pray, for all those who have brought me, and brought us, to this present moment in time. Here I pray for all those who have taken part in making me who I am today.

You are here with me in this dark, cool cellar of my youth.

4 : 3 0   A M

In this cellar, Father, I find all I need to make that special bread of the Eucharist and give thanks to You. I take this bread and wine and I say, "This is my Body. This is my Blood."

J e s u s   i s   w i t h   u s   i n   o u r   c e l l a r s . *Together we pray to You with the words Your Son taught us: "Our Father . . ."*

With Your holy nourishment, we find the strength to ask pardon of all our sins: the sins of youth, the sins of young adulthood, and the sins that we remember as we grow older. Forgive us, Father; forgive us, as we now forgive those who in any way have offended us.

We know that You have invited us to enter into this cellar to be with You. We have nothing to fear for You are with us. You are our loving Father providing for our daily needs. With Jesus as our brother, we have confidence to now call You, Father.

II

Encountering God
in the Darkness

In chapter one I ventured to go into the cellar of my youth to face my hidden fears and then expose them to "Our Father." My hope was that you would also venture into your childhood and let your hidden fears come forth, bringing them to the Father for healing.

Now, we are about to go on to another level of prayer. St. John of the Cross calls this "the dark night." For some strange reason, this invitation to enter into the darkness is also a process that will prepare us to encounter the light. But, first we are challenged to really enter into the darkness.

At this stage of the journey, I would encourage you, my reader, to keep a spiritual journal, just as I am doing now. Your fears will not be the same as mine. Simply jot them down and see where they take you.

It was only by entering into the darkest part of the cellar that I was able to let go and write of fears I would normally not express even to my closest friends. I invite you to come along with me and enter into that secret chamber, that cellar. Follow me down into the cellar and see what happens. But be sure to leave the lights off, let your fears come forward, and share them with God, "Our Father," who made us and loves us.

4 : 3 0   A M

The invitation comes from You, Father, to descend into the cellar of my youth and there to remain in the darkness of the night. You are now asking me to go down into the cellar without turning on the lights. Your Son, Jesus, tells us in Matthew to go into the storeroom, the cellar, to go through the door and then lock it and pray to You, the One who sees and knows everything that takes place in secret. But it really seems strange that You should insist I not turn on the lights. I will obey Your will, but it really does not make much sense.

I n   t h e   d a y s   o f   J e s u s   they did not have electric lights, as we do today. I can remember the light fixtures when I was a small boy. The lower part of the fixture held an electric bulb and the upper portion had a globe within which was a fine, cylinder wick that glowed whenever the gas was turned on and lit.

I also remember during the years I spent in Africa that we often had to rely on a standby generator that was cranked up at sunset and turned off whenever the monks or nuns went to bed. Someone was assigned to crank up the generator whenever it was time to get up, about 3 AM, for the vigil prayer service. I would leave the light switch on in my room, and in the morning when the light came on, I knew it was time to rise.

You, Father, are now inviting me to descend into the cellar without turning on the lights. Don't You know that as a small boy I was afraid to go into dark places? In fact, I was afraid to even go to bed because of the darkness. But now You ask me to do this freely to enter into the darkness of this cellar?

What really is the value of this darkness? Darkness is the absence of light; light makes everything visible; but here I am in this darkness.

It was Zelie, mother of St. Thérèse of Lisieux, who wrote of her stubborn child: "You could put her in the cellar for a whole day and she would spend the night there rather than saying yes." I'm afraid that I would rather say yes than remain in this dark cellar. While in France several years ago, serving as chaplain to the Lay Cistercians of this community, I visited that cellar where Thérèse preferred to stay rather than say her yes.

But I've gone this far, I might as well give it a try and see where it takes me. Okay, here goes. I go through the door, shut, and lock it. Now I have to find my way down these steps in the dark. Down I go, feeling the stone wall with my fingertips. Here I am in this cellar alone with all these jars, but I can't see a thing. *This doesn't make any sense to me, but I will sit in obedience to Your invitation to enter into this night.*

4 : 3 0   P M

I find myself in the corner of this Abbey church and once again You invite me to lock the door, walk past the light switch without turning it on, and feel my way along as I descend the steps into this cellar to pray to You. Here I sit, waiting in the darkness of this night. How easy it would be to flick on the light in order to see, but I won't.

I a m r e m i n d e d of an event from more than twenty years ago. It was January 1982. It was about 1 PM and I was reading the Christmas mail that had arrived late in Abakaliki, Nigeria. The newly constructed monastery was wired for electricity, but we had to depend on a generator that was turned on only at sunset. The monastery was built only a few hundred yards from the main high-power lines going from Enugu to the Cameroon border. Without a transformer, we were unable to tap into this source of electrical power. As I was reading my Christmas mail, I saw the outlet box give off a bright light and then begin to smoke. The fuse box outside my room exploded and began smoldering. I ran over to the main monastery and Mother Margaret Mary said the light bulb over her head had just exploded and fuse boxes around the building were smoldering.

Father Andrew and I rushed into the city of Abakaliki to N.E.P.A., Nigerian Electric Power Authority, often referred to as "No Electrical Power at All." The authorities there said that it was impossible for electrical power to be in our line; we were worrying for no reason. And so, we all returned to the monastery to examine the situation again. There, at the foot of the transformer, was a dead snake that had made contact with the high power line and sent that high-powered surge of electricity through the monastery.

Here I sit in this cellar with electricity, but the switch is off in obedience to You, Father.

4 : 3 0   A M

A s   I   s i t   a l o n e   in the darkness of this cellar, I know that I am not alone. A letter recently arrived from Mildred, a former childhood classmate of mine. I had written to her and shared my experience of praying in the cellar. She wrote back and described an experience and feelings that are unfortunately all-too-common.

"Thank you for sharing with me the ideas of 'praying in the cellar.' I could relate to the cellar of your youth, and I did join you. It took me back to my youth—some of it was happy and a lot of it was frightening. Dad had an alcohol addiction, and it made our lives pretty miserable. I didn't experience a father's love, but I realize now that he didn't know how much it hurt us. I have asked my Father in heaven to give him peace and a place of rest. I didn't realize how much I loved him until he died. I also asked my heavenly Father to forgive me for all of the times I have hurt my father and mother, and my children and spouse. I have so much to ask forgiveness for."

Indeed, our earthly fathers at times fall short of making known what fatherhood is all about. By going to You, we discover that You indeed are Father. I know, Father, that not all of our earthly fathers love as they should, or care for us as they should. But let us bring our experiences in relationships to You for healing and Your divine love.

4 : 3 0   A M

F a t h e r ,   I realize some homes do not have cellars. My brother Joe kept everything in his garage. For some people, it might be the attic or some closet that are the secret places where things are stored away until the day that they are once again needed. Sometimes it is only after our death that others will discover all the junk that we have accumulated over the years.

What will others find in my room after my death? Will they throw away things that I might have kept? What will they do with all the old class notes? What about those booklets made from old envelopes with notes written on them from when I was a novice some fifty-five years ago? Some of these notes are now turning yellow.

I am reminded of when old Brother Clement died in 1964 and the abbot, Dom Augustine, opened up the drawer where brother kept all his private notes and behold, his notes were being eaten up by silverfish. Here in the Deep South, silverfish thrive on old notes, they even devour library books.

4 : 3 0   A M

I just do not like sitting in this darkness. But to you, Father, darkness is as light.

A g a i n , I am reminded of 1982 when I was recovering from hepatitis B. During the night I would awake in the dormitory of the Monastery of Awhum to hear the other monks snoring. The dorm was pitch black, and I was afraid of the dark. The blackness of the night filled me with fear, and reasoning about it did not help. I had to beg the brothers to leave the candle burning during the night. That was one way to cope.

Now you ask me to face my fear of darkness. Could it be that I fear blindness because my two brothers experienced blindness? Francis and Sal started to go blind in their thirties, and even now, I marvel at Francis's fortitude in the midst of his darkness. (My brother Sal has died.)

4 : 3 0   A M

M y   f r i e n d   C o n n i e   phoned yesterday to say that my writings were making her very hungry for some good Italian cooking. She went out and bought bottles of oregano and basil. She suggested that I write an Italian cookbook. Northern Italians cook differently than those of us from the South. They use much more hot red pepper and a lot more polenta, which is similar to southern grits. Sicilian cooking is milder.

How could I write a cookbook that says add a dash of this and a pinch of that and cook it until it is ready? I am not a cook who follows recipes very closely. Good cooking also involves other things, such as knowing how long the dish should sit before it is served. A good dish of pasta is great when first cooked. Here at the monastery it is cooked an hour or so ahead of time and then put into a hot box. After the noonday, special prayer, Angelus, the pasta is placed on the serving line and by the time the abbot has said grace and the monks get through the line, the food is getting cold. It is still good, but nothing like Mama used to make.

Sometimes even a good cook will need another person to help decide what missing element is needed. The other day the abbot came into the kitchen while I was cooking and I asked him to taste the soup to see what it needed. His reply was, "It needs to be thrown out." That was one of his jokes. In truth, the soup passed inspection since it contained some of the leftover soup he had made from the day before.

I remember reading from a cookbook that said soup gets better as it gets older. However, sometimes it can get so old that it is ready for the slop bucket—good only for feeding to the pigs.

The hardest part about cooking is the cleanup—doing the pots and pans. Our former abbot Dom Bernard was notorious for using almost every pot and pan in the kitchen whenever he cooked. He made up for this by helping to clean up.

Preparing food is a large part of living, and yet I can see why St. Paul suggested to the Corinthians that the Eucharist be separated from the meal since we can get so absorbed in our food that we forget about Christ, the guest of honor.

4 : 3 0   A M

F a t h e r , in the darkness of this cellar I am still thinking of food. Those French nuns at *L'abbaye Cistercienne de Grandselve*

(French for "Cistercian Abbey of the Great Forest"), in the jungles of the Cameroons, really knew how to cook. From my personal experience, I know that the French have as natural an instinct for cooking as do the Sicilians. They are able to throw anything together and have it become a good soup.

While in the Cameroon, I was the English-speaking chaplain to seven Nigerian novices. My friend, Pere Giles, was the chaplain to the French-speaking nuns of the community. At the dinner table, Pere and I communicated with the help of a French-English dictionary sitting between us. The nuns made sure to put out the wine bottle and the wine vinegar and olive oil for the salad between us, as well. To me, there is nothing that can take the place of vinegar and olive oil for a good salad. I also like the Greek addition of olives and cheese. We ate well, as our French hosts did such a great job in preparing our meals.

Our hosts made sure that the chaplains did not remain vegetarian by having meat on the table. We often had chicken. One day, it was brought to my attention that the hens that died during the night were cooked for the chaplains the following day. I lost my taste for chicken, but not for the fresh French bread.

I kept encouraging the Nigerians to learn how to cook from the French nuns, for we were soon to depart to establish a foundation at Abakaliki, Nigeria. Once the foundation was made, the quality of the food changed. Some foods cooked by the Ibo nuns were not to my taste. *Garri*, made of ground-up cassava that looks a lot like an oversized, white, sweet potato, has to be processed to remove the tannic acid, and then fried to dry. It is then added to boiling water to make a paste similar to grits or polenta. Dough balls are formed by hand, dipped into a slimy or oily substance such as okra, or palm oil, and then swallowed whole—no chewing, just swallowed.

The sausage termites swarmed twice each year. When this happened, the nuns went outside to gather up the termites, throwing them into water which made the wings come off. These wingless creatures were then fried in palm oil. The natives as well as the German shepherds loved them. I was bold enough to taste them once and have to admit that they were not that bad. But, I was never bold enough to try the cooked caterpillars.

The fruits of the tropics are a different story. Mangoes are my favorite. The German mangoes were about six inches in length and shaped like footballs. When green they are as hard as a rock. Why they are called *German* I do not know. I once asked Donatus, a close friend of mine, who had one wife in the village and another in the city of Abakaliki, to climb the tree at the bishop's house to shake loose the fruit. He did his job so well that one hit me right on the top of my head. For a moment I saw stars.

Perhaps the hardest food to stomach was the bitter leaf. These leaves were picked from a tree and cooked like spinach. They are worse than eating green persimmons, so bitter are they, and yet the natives loved them. They claimed bitter leaf was good for killing the worms in the stomach. (Or was it the malaria?) They also eat a lot of hot pepper which they also claim kills worms. I found it just as easy to take worm medicine whenever I got that strange gnawing feeling in my stomach.

4 : 3 0   A M

F a t h e r ,   what good can come from me sitting in this night? During my time here, the fears of my childhood surface and here I am supposed to be a grown-up. I face fears that go beyond reason. Zechariah says that God will "'give light to those who live in darkness and the shadow of death.'" Here I sit in the shadow of death but see nothing coming from all of this as I face myself in this lonely purgatory of memories. *Is this Your gift to me as the past becomes present? What is happening?*

What is this light for which I am waiting in the darkness? Is my belief in You the beginning of the light? St. Elizabeth of the Trinity defines faith as the face-to-face encounter with God in the night. Is this what I am now doing in Your presence as I sit in this darkness—facing You head on?

I hear the truck outside the Abbey church here to pick up the trash. I am reminded of my first visit to the Cameroons. I was waiting at the border for a ride, but my ride was late in arriving. An Englishman offered me a lift in his small Volkswagen "Beetle." We began our trip on the international highway that joins East to West Africa. It was only a dirt road cut into the jungle.

As we were about to begin our ascent of the Cameroon Mountains, we saw a sign that read: "Proceed at your own risk. Horn at all bends. Your life is in your own hands!" Despite the sign, we proceeded up that mountain.

In the tropics, nightfall comes quickly and before we knew it, it was dark. Still, we slowly drove on up the mountain. The road was filled with potholes, and every so often I had to get out to see if the Volkswagen would make it. My English friend thought it was about time to look for shelter for the evening.

I asked, "Where are we going to find shelter around here?"

He replied, "There must be a Catholic Mission around here someplace."

And so we kept driving into the night, looking for somewhere to stop and sleep. Every so often we passed a mud hut with a thatched roof and a small fire burning just inside the door. We would stop and ask if there was a Catholic Mission near by and the reply was again and again, "Up, up."

Finally, at about 10:30, we arrived at a small village named Widekum and sure enough, there was a Mission Church. We startled the Dutch missionary out of bed. He cranked up his generator and gave us rooms for the night. *I was thankful to You, Father, for providing a bed for that night.* I am wondering how many people have to live in the streets for the night with no place to lay their heads.

4 : 3 0   A M

I l o c k t h e d o o r and once again descend to sit in this dark cellar. *Am I hearing You correctly? Surely You don't want me to get up and go into that banana room and remain there with all my fears! If You are a God of Love, how could You ask me to do something like this? In there, I will never see the light coming in the upper window since there is no window. No, God, not this!*

Well, alright God, if You insist, I might as well also give this a try. In I go and close the door.

My brother Joe was locked in this same room for talking back to Dad, but I am here because You want me here, Father, not because I have talked back to You.

Since I've locked the upper door coming into the cellar, I see no reason for locking this one, too. Who would ever want to come into this banana room and sit here with me? But also, I feel like asking: What did I do to deserve this? Even here I am not alone. Hundreds, thousands, millions of others have preceded me into this night. Helpless, we sit here in this tomb, in this night, waiting.

In this early hour I hear the whistle of the train in the town of Conyers, not far from the Abbey. Next, I hear the blower trying to push some heat into the chill of this Abbey church on a cold January morning; it fails to warm me up.

Alone I sit in this banana room and yet I am not alone. Hi, Joe! What are you doing here? So this is the place where Dad locked you up whenever you talked back to him. You would have been better off if you would have kept your mouth shut like the rest of us kids, but you were always unique. It is not too bad in here as long as you remain with me. You had a big brother who let you out whenever Papa was not looking. Will my big brother also get me out of here? *Jesus, where are You?*

4 : 3 0   A M

T h e   L i t u r g y   today contemplated the Baptism of Jesus. As I sit in the banana room, I think of a swimming pool. Old St. Joseph's Hospital in downtown Atlanta had just been remodeled and Dom Augustine was invited to consecrate the new altar. He invited me to go along as his Master of Ceremonies. Afterwards, the hospital superior gave us a tour of the renovated building. In the basement, they had just constructed a swimming pool.

Down we went and entered a dark room. The supervisor said to us, "Be careful, for there's a swimming pool over there." We waited in the darkness for some time, and then I began to move about slowly. My foot went down and my two hands went out and I caught hold of something. The lights went on and I was looking down into a fifteen-foot empty swimming pool. My right leg was down in the corner and my two hands were holding onto the two edges of the corner. I backed away with a prayer of gratitude to my guardian angel for protecting me from a painful fall. A few inches in any other direction and I surely would have tumbled in headlong. Yes, I knew my angel was near at hand.

As I sit alone in this banana room, my angel is at my side to watch over me and protect me from all evil, even from the empty swimming pool in the night.

4 : 3 0   A M

A part of me now looks forward to locking the door, descending the steps, and being with You, God, in the darkness of this banana room. But still, another part of me can hardly wait to get out.

T h e   g r e e n   b u n c h e s   of bananas in this room cannot be eaten. In fact, they cannot even be seen. All I am able to do is reach out and touch them with my imagination. Even here I am not secure, for fear there may be a spider hidden in one of the bunches.

I am reminded of the fears that I had as a child, not wanting to go to bed and be alone in that dark. There were those strange spots on the wall of my room. In those days of the Great Depression, there were no night-lights.

Aunt Rose was the only one who would stay with me in my room until I fell asleep.

Here I sit in this banana room surfacing those fears of my past. *Here I sit in this Abbey church with You, Father. With You I will not fear, for You are a father of love and light as I sit in this darkness.*

4 : 3 0   A M

D o w n   I   g o   and here I am in this banana room. I recall the days of World War II when there were "dim-outs" and "blackouts." All street lights were turned off and driving at night was forbidden. All lights burning within a house had to be shaded so that they could not be seen from the road, otherwise we would get into trouble for violating the mandatory blackout. Entire cities became invisible in the darkness of the night. *I am invisible with You.*

As I sit in the darkness of this room, I wonder if there are invisible cities all around me. I do not have the eyes to behold the angels in their God-given glory about me. What is it like on the other side—on the side of heaven—as I sit in this darkness?

4 : 3 0   A M

A l o n e   in this darkness I wait with You, Father. Are there cellars in Your Being filled with provisions that someday You will bring to light? What are those hidden chambers filled with Your love? When creation began, You opened up only one of those cellars that we might see and say with You, "It is good! It is very good!"

Male and female did You create them, that I might be a part of that creation in this moment of time.

The heart of Your Son, Jesus, is a cellar to us. You make known those hidden chambers in those cellars of Your Love. I sit in the midst of this cellar of Your Being, in the darkness of this night.

What is this that is now happening? As I sit in the darkness, I now feel as though the room is filled with light, for You are here. In this darkness, I am surrounded with love. What is love? You are Love.

God is love! I am lost in the cellar of Love.

Love is not an attraction that ends only in a sexual expression of one's being. Sex is only one means by which we continue God's creation on earth. *In that day when creation is completed, sex will cease to be, but God's love will always be, for You, God, are love. Within Your Being we will find the meaning of it all. Only then will be the beginning, the beginning of love. Until then, I wait in the darkness of this night with You.*

It is only by my first entering into the dark chambers of my being, into this oh-so-dark banana room, that I am now able to encounter the fullness of Your light, Your love. Psalm 139 expresses what I am trying to say:

Where could I go to escape your Spirit?

Where could I flee from your presence? If I climb the heavens, you are there;

there, too, if I lie in Sheol. *If I go up the Cameroonian mountains, You are there.*

If I go down to the darkest recesses of this cellar,
You are even present there.
For You, darkness itself is not dark,
and night shines as the day;
darkness and light are the same.

7 : 4 0   P M

I sit in the Abbey church before the Exposed Sacrament, Jesus, our eucharistically present Lord. *For half an hour here I have tried to enter into the banana room to sit in Your presence.* How difficult it can sometimes be to enter into silence at the end of the day!

The events of the past day come to remind me of the times I have tried to suppress my irritability at myself and others. I am reminded of the times when things have not gone according to my plans. As I try to enter into the darkness to find the light, I am hindered because I continue to recall the events of the day. It is much easier for me to enter into prayer in the early hours of the morning than now. *Have mercy on me, O Lord, have mercy on me.*

4 : 3 0   A M

The blower turns on to send heat into the church. Now I can begin to write without fear of disturbing my brother monks in prayer.

A good night of sleep has recreated, renewed, refreshed, emptied me of the anxieties of yesterday. *In this early hour I come before You to be filled, Father, with Your Being and love. To be in Your presence is like sunbathing on a beach and feeling the radiance of sunlight, and yet this is January and I am in this cool Abbey.*

A letter arrived from my first cousin, Josie (Josephine), the other day. She wrote of Babi, our grandfather: "He always frightened me," she said. I am sorry that Josie experienced grandfather as a man to be feared, because I didn't feel that way.

I was only six years old when I came to know the good side of Babi. It seemed he did not know a word of English although he had been in America for many years. I was in Saltsburg for the carnival but had no money. My other first cousins, Baby Joe, and his brother, Francis, knew how to get money from Babi, and they taught me how to do it. I went up to granddad and said: "Babi, *soldi?*" (*Soldi* is Sicilian for money.) He reached into his pocket and pulled out a handful of change and handed me a dime. That is what grandfathers are all about! The following year Babi was kidnapped by the Mafia and died of a stroke.

So many fears, Father. The darkness of the cellar forces me to remember those phone calls Dad received from the Mafia. They were calling from Vandergrift, Pennsylvania, offering "protection" if we paid up. By that time Dad had sold the fruit and vegetable business and was in the movie theater business. Papa refused to compromise with the Mafia. My brothers Anthony and Joe went to bed at night with the gun in the drawer between their twin beds. I was only eleven, and slept with Joe. I was told to keep my distance from strangers, for fear that I would be kidnapped. When strangers came into our little town of Avonmore, I ran in the other direction.

Years later, in about 1977, I was assigned to be the retreat master of the guesthouse in Conyers. When visitors came into the guesthouse—which, of course, they always did!—I instinctively wanted to run in the other direction. I had to learn to overcome my fears. After my return from Africa, in about 1988, I was made guestmaster for the monastery. Even to this day I have to face this fear of visitors that is hidden deep within me.

4 : 3 0   A M

Here I am supposed to be in prayer to You, Father, and I am wondering how I spent that dime at the carnival. If I remember correctly, I debated within myself whether to buy a shiny, maroon candy apple or a large puff of cotton-candy. I believe the apple won out. Just this morning at vigils, the Genesis account of the Fall of my mother Eve was read. She also chose the fruit of a tree, and here I am with my fallen nature inherited from father Adam and mother Eve, yet redeemed by the fruit of the tree of life, Your Son, Jesus Christ.

You continue to speak with me as You spoke in that garden to my first parents. You speak to me through Jesus and Your common Spirit as I sit in the darkness of this banana room. Here I have discovered in this darkness the hidden chambers of Your love. You tested me by inviting me to enter into this darkness where I have discovered Your light. From this hidden darkness I ponder on the possibility of other cellars that may reveal more of the greatness of Your love. You test us and our freedom to love You and You invite us to enter into Your kingdom. If this creation is so full of wonder, and yet it can be compared to a cellar; how much more can we expect when beholding the vastness of Your being, You who are the creator of all. Then, as Your hidden chambers turn into heavenly kingdoms, You will open up to us the fullness and vastness of Your castle—many floors of building upon this simple cellar—each made up of all three of You: Father, Son, and Spirit of Love.

T h e   w o r l d   seems to be telling me that I am wasting my time here. I should go out and enjoy life. *On the other hand, You do invite me to close and lock the door to be alone with You in the darkness of this banana room, and, I am beginning to love it!*

4 : 3 0 A M

*The Book of Genesis is being read to us at the end of the first
nocturn of vigils. You, Father, are a God of questions. You asked
questions of Adam and Eve, and of Cain. "Where is your brother?
What have you done?" You continue to ask questions of each of
us. Questions! Questions! Questions!*

*You ask questions in order to see if we know the right answer.
You ask to get us to think, don't You? You already know the
answers. You are the Master, we the disciples; You are the teacher,
we the students; You are the Father, we the children. This is the
dialogue of prayer. Speak Lord! I am listening.*

*I sit in the darkest recesses of this cellar, in this banana room,
waiting now for Your questions. Speak Lord! I am listening.*

T h e   r a i n   f a l l s   on the roof of this Abbey
church as I listen.

"Where are your brothers?" *You know the answer to that
question better than I do. Some of my older brothers are too old
to get up at this early hour. They would probably like to be here
with You if they could, but they are with You in a special way
through their suffering.*

*Some of my brothers are scattered throughout this Abbey church
in prayer to You, just as I am. Those whose bodies are resting in
the cemetery just behind this church are most probably in Your
eternal embrace of love. Perhaps a few are in that place of waiting that is called Purgatory, and for them we pray. My two
blood brothers, Francis and Sal, both lived most of their lives in
blindness and in their darkness, they were alone with You. My
Ibo brother monks in Nigeria are probably at work with the
poultry and in the fields. Here I am with You, Father, waiting
for You to ask questions and by Your silence I feel You are
pleased with my sitting in silence with You.*

4 : 3 0   A M

Now it is my turn to ask You some questions since You are not asking questions of me. Here goes. As I sit in this banana room with these green bunches all around me, I would like to know: Why is it that the word "banana" does not appear in the Bible? Bananas are one of the most important fruits in the modern world. A bunch of bananas weighs anywhere from fifty to one hundred and twenty-five pounds. Over one hundred million bunches are shipped each year. That is a lot of bananas! "Did Jesus ever eat a banana?" I have a feeling He must have eaten bananas when He was a small boy in Egypt. I can imagine Him blessing the bananas and saying: "Increase, multiply, and fill the earth." His prayer has come true, and here I am sitting in this room with these bananas, and they are all too green to eat.

T h e   w o r d   b a n a n a   is an African word. I wonder if the English word banana is related to the Arabic word baba, which means father? Is there a reason that my grandfather whom we called Babianni has hidden within this name the word banan? Papa was called by the men in the streets, "Joe Banan."

I have many questions, Father, and I am glad that I may talk with You as with a friend. The other day, Bob Wilcox, a friend of the monastery, was called in to study our bonsai tree business. We were discussing some problems related to administration. At one point Bob asked, "What would Jesus do?"

"Good question," I said, "but I think the question ought to be put another way: 'What does Jesus want me to do?'"

Jesus is now with You in glory and He is leaving it up to me to do as He would do and to love as He would love. Even if I "fail" in the eyes of the world, it is up to You to decide whether or not I really failed in Your will.

There is more to life than being successful. There are great lessons to be learned from our failures. Life is filled with a lot of blunders and mistakes. *The most important thing to remember is to constantly try and walk before You as Noah did, and to always seek to do Your will, no matter what that may entail, like going into the darkness of a banana room.*

Genesis 6 shows You, Father, regretting that You made us. Even You made mistakes, but then there was Noah. Without Noah, I would not be before You today. He walked before You and did Your will while others laughed. Am I doing Your will today? Am I concerned about what others are thinking of me? Do I listen to Your Spirit dwelling within my heart? Questions, questions, questions. What is this life all about?

4:30 AM

On this Sunday, I have come to this corner of the Abbey church after hearing the story of the Flood (Genesis 7). From here, I am going down into the banana cellar to face the fears of my youth. *Here I sit ready to uncover another great fear from my childhood days—the desire that You gave me for the love of the opposite sex. What are these strong impulses I continue to find within myself? Are they not also gifts from You?*

Male and female did You make us and the attraction that we have to each other is Your gift. I recall falling in love with Mary Ann in the third grade. In the fourth grade, I sat in the front seat of the second row on the right, and Mary Ann sat in the front seat of the third row. We wrote love letters to each other. I would write a note, crumple it up, let it fall on the floor and then cough to get her attention. She would then bend over to tie her shoestring and pick up the crumpled note. This is the manner in which we exchanged love notes.

Once I was bold enough to write: "Dear Mary Ann, when we grow up will you marry me? Love, Luigene."

The note was crumpled and fell to the floor. She tied her shoe, picked up the note and read it. It seemed like an eternity before I got that response. I stooped to the floor to tie my shoestring, picked up the note and read: "Dear Luigene, when we grow up I cannot marry you because you are a Catholic."

My dream world came to an end. What does being a Catholic have to do with getting married, I wondered? Mary Ann moved to New York City after the fourth grade and my whole world came to an end. During the fifth grade, I went to Mass on the first Friday of the month for nine months praying for her return.

Here I am, sixty-five plus years later, waiting for that prayer to be answered. *Maybe You, Father, have some secrets in store as Mary Ann and I encounter each other in Your eternal embrace. The only thing I know for certain is that she became a Jehovah's Witness later in life. May her zeal somehow bring us into the eternal embrace of Your love.*

4 : 3 0 A M

Here in this darkness, I make known to You, Father, all my fears in respect to sexuality. Nothing is hidden from You and to You I come to expose my wounds and ask for healing. You are indeed the Author of my being as I am. Before You I come to ask pardon for those times I have tried to hide from love, as well as for those times that I have not loved according to Your will.

I simply remain where I am in this darkness and bask in the radiance of Your healing light. Male and female did You make us and You looked down upon Your creation and saw that it was very good; then came the Fall. Sexuality is positive and beautiful as it originally came from Your hand, but without You, it loses all of its beauty.

4 : 3 0 A M

G o d i s L o v e but human love is a mystery. *Now that I have spoken before You, Father, of my puppy love, I will uncover another early love of mine. I want to share these with You.*

Marilyn and I dated in high school and during our first year of college. She was in Pittsburgh and I was in Washington, D.C., when her "Dear John" letter arrived in my mail. Since she was so far away she thought it best to break off the relationship. In the next mail, she returned my class ring, which I had given her to wear while we were apart. Suppressing all emotion, I simply admitted to the reality of the situation. Life had to go on.

Thirty-seven years later, I found myself in the Cameroons beginning my new role as chaplain to a group of nuns. One evening, Sister Gerard turned off the generator and I was in the darkness of my room in the guesthouse. It was time to go to bed, and I was in the dark as I am now in this banana room. Climbing under the mosquito netting, I fell asleep and had a dream.

In that dream, my childhood buddies came to me and said: "Lui, we have found a guru, and he can give you the answer to anything you want to know." I thought and then said: "I want to know about love."

At once Marilyn appeared to me in that dream and said, "Every other woman will treat you as I did."

I woke up suddenly in that dark room and realized how much it hurt to break off that relationship so many years earlier. In the dream, I actually heard her voice and it helped me to realize that the wound of suppressed emotions had to finally be lanced. I began to weep as years of pent-up emotions were being released. I was being liberated by that dream. Afterwards, I finally felt free to approach women without the fear of being rejected. Now, I could become a chaplain to these nuns as someone not afraid of love. *Thank You, Father, for that liberating dream.*

Other loves entered into my life in those years, but none of the same importance as those first two. First, there was Mary Ann. Second, there was Marilyn. But my greatest love is for another woman named Mary. She, who is the mother of Your Son, Jesus, is also my mother and the Mother of Your Church. At the end of each monastic day at the service of compline we Cistercians turn to her as we sing our "Salve" to her who is "Our light, our sweetness, and our hope."

4 : 3 0   A M

H e r e   I   s i t ,   having surfaced most of the fears of my youth. One final fear I need to face—far removed from my childhood by the grace of God—is the fear of dying. I must now face the inevitable.

This is not the fear of the past but of the present and the future. I see my friends falling apart and soon my turn will come. Thus far I have celebrated the funeral Mass and burial of Dad, Mom, Josephine, Anthony, Joe, even that of my sister, Catherine, and most recently my brother, Sal. Who will be next? Will it be me? My other brother, Francis, recently told me that he had a dream in which Catherine told him he would be the last of us to die, at age eighty-six. Francis is now eighty-three. (He reminded me that this was only a dream!)

How can I fear the unknown, Father, since I know that You are beyond all that I fear. Doesn't wine get better as it gets older? Do I expect to get better as I get older? I doubt it, but does it really matter? I am who I am in You, God.

I have entered this banana room at Your invitation, Father, and now I feel the invitation of Your Holy Spirit to enter into the aging and the dying process without fear. I go from this banana room into the tomb of death to there await with Jesus, Your Son, the summons to come forth into the Dawn. Slowly my faculties have begun to fall apart—my hearing, my vision, my memory—what's next? All this precedes me as I prepare to enter into the night of death and there to await the Dawn. As the saying goes, "The night is darkest just before the dawn."

Here, Father, I trust in Your mercy.

Here, brother Jesus, I trust in Your compassion.

Here, Holy Spirit, I rest in Your abiding love.

To enter into the darkness of Your Being is to see the light.

4 : 3 0   A M

It is my prayer that others will rise at this early hour to enter into this darkness and be strengthened and enlightened for the coming of the day.

May mothers come before You, Father, while their children are asleep and may they be strengthened to better nurture and care for those that they love. May they remain before You in this darkness and silence to experience the light of Your love, the warmth of Your presence.

Before You, may their fears surface and be exposed. May they hear You say: "Fear not, for I am with You. Fear not, for I am in You. Fear not for I love You. Fear not, for I am your Father who made you and love you. Fear not, but come before me and pray that prayer taught to you by My own eternal Son. Pray: 'Our Father, who art in heaven . . .'"

You have made all that was and is and is to come. It is You who made and make the galaxies. You are the author of it all. This creation is indeed the work of Your hand. In it and through it you expose to us many little chambers of Your cellar, Your hiddenness, Your cellar filled with Love.

Here I pray, we pray, for all those who have brought me, and brought us, to this present moment in time. Here I pray for all those who have taken part in making me who I am today.

You give to each and every seed planted in the earth the power to do Your will. You feed us and care for all our needs. "Thy will be done on earth as it is in heaven." You are here with me in this dark, cool cellar of my youth.

You have invited us to enter this cellar. We have nothing to fear, for You are with us. You are our loving Father providing for our daily needs. With Jesus as our brother, we have confidence to now call You Father.

4 : 3 0 A M

" ' I , i n m y t u r n , have seen the one who sees me.'" These words of Hagar are very descriptive of a mystical experience. *You are a God who sees all. You see the future of Ishmael for nothing is hidden from You. And now, I can begin to see You, too.*

III

Encountering God in the Light

In some parts of Africa, pidgin
English was introduced because of the large variety of
native languages. The readings of the liturgy were also
done in pidgin. In it, God the Father is called *Papa God*.
After the proclamation of the words of Scripture, the reader
says, "God, He talk." Indeed, God does talk to us.

Some people seem to rush into contemplation before
they are ready for this mode of prayer. To pray, yes, but to

pray with contemplative prayer depends on God's gift to you. St. Bernard holds that the first step to knowing God is to know oneself. To know yourself, you must first remember from whence you have come and what has been. Remember, remember, remember!

God invites us to remember: "'Then you will remember your evil conduct and actions. You will loathe yourselves for your sins . . .'" In his *Rule*, St. Benedict calls this process "compunction," which literally means to tear apart the heart through introspection and repentance. This is the first step to any kind of prayer.

During the Last Supper, Jesus took bread and wine and said, "This is my body. This is my blood." Jesus also said, "Do this in remembrance of me." To Jews (and remember that Jesus was a Jew), "to remember" is a very significant term. If we study *remember* as found in the Bible, we discover that the Hebrews remember the actions of God in the past that God might now, in this moment, become present. We, in turn, by recalling the past, do so in order to ask God to become present and to heal those memories of the past.

Imagine a mother trying to enter into deep contemplative prayer in her bedroom while the children are crying, the supper is burning on the kitchen stove, the smoke detector is going off, and the phone is ringing. Our first reaction would be, "Hey, stop! First things have to come first." In the same way, one is not ready for real contemplative prayer until the house is at peace. If distractions keep coming during prayer, this may be an indication that something within the house needs attending to first. Once the house is at rest, and all the distracting noises quiet down, then we are ready to enter another mode of prayer. Then, we are ready to enter into contemplative prayer.

With this third chapter, I continue to go into the cellar to pray. But now I hear God's invitation to turn on the lights. I invite you to continue with me in the journey of learning to pray this way.

If you are like me, you may have grown tired of using your memory and imagination to go into the cellar. I have grown somewhat tired of that banana room with its memories of my past. So, in this chapter, I begin to simply sit in the darkness of the Abbey church and ponder on the Scripture being read at the end of the first nocturn of vigils. You should do the same, using the words of a daily Scripture reading as your guide.

The words of Scripture present themes to me, and I reflect on them. You will do the same, both with my Scripture readings and reflections, and through your own. Have your Bible handy and use my reflections as starting points for your own prayer with the Father. Many times, however, we must simply sit in God's presence and wait. Join with me in the Abbey and together let us ponder and reflect on the Word. "For God, He talk."

IT IS GOOD TO PRAY IN THE LIGHT

4 : 3 0   A M

Father, what is going on here? Now that I am getting comfortable sitting in the security of this dark banana room, You invite me to turn on the lights. I seem to hear You say, "I want to look upon My creation through your eyes. I want to see the cellar through your eyes." Will you let me do this?

O k a y , on goes the light switch. No longer do I have to feel the wall or count the steps like my blind brother,

Francis, and no longer will I sit in darkness filled with memories of the past.

But I cannot leave the cellar of my past entirely behind. I can see the steps and down we go. There in front of us is the basket for the dirty laundry that has to be sorted by color to be washed on Monday morning. There is the old stove that Mom used to cook down the tomatoes. To the left of the stove hangs the pizzelle mold made of cast iron, and to the right the hot water heater. During the Depression, the hot water heater was lit on Saturday morning, since everyone was expected to take a bath or shower in preparation for Sunday. Next to the heater is the box of spaghetti, the flour tin, and the jug of wine vinegar. There is the old kitchen cabinet. Gee, I haven't thought of that kitchen cabinet for years. Across from it, in the other corner, is the small room with the commode and sink.

4 : 3 0   A M

Now that You have invited me to turn on the lights, I find that I am no longer drawn to this cellar as a fearful place. Now it seems to be an ordinary place with nothing to fear. I see the jars of tomato sauce, the wine barrel, and the other things here, but I now see it all with the lights turned on. How different it is to have light shining where once I was afraid. You have turned on these lights and I thank You, Father. Instead of praying in the cellar, I am now inclined simply to sit in this monastery church and ponder the Scriptures that have just been read to us monks at this early hour.

(Genesis 25) Rebekah has twins fighting within her womb. She consults with You, Father, and You reply by saying "'There are

two nations in your womb, your issue will be two rival peoples.'" *Questions! Where did Rebekah go when she needed to consult with You? Did she go to her storeroom as I am now in this cellar with You?*

Who are You, O God, who knows the future of nations before they are born? Do You also know my future? Do You already see me on my deathbed? Do You already see me in Your eternal Now? How can this be? And yet I know it is. You are a God who sees all in Your eternal Now *and yet You are hidden from me. With the freedom You now give me I fall before You.*

Did You see me before I was born and already know what I would become? Did You see me scribbling those notes to Mary Ann and also know that I would someday be writing to You in the darkness of this Abbey church as I am right now? You saw me in my mother's womb and knew then what I would become. You saw me and still see me. Before You, a hidden God, I fall and plead for mercy from Your love. Through this chapter of Genesis, You have spoken to me today.

4 : 3 0   A M

(G e n e s i s   2 8)   Does the ladder appearing in Jacob's dream in Genesis symbolize the humanity of Jesus? Are the seven rungs of the ladder God's many means of grace toward us?

I remember when I was a little boy hearing my bigger brothers playing basketball in the top of the barn. The barn door was open, and I went in to discover a ladder going to the upper loft. Being too small to climb that ladder, I cried out to my brothers and someone came down to help me up into that new world above. In former days, hay was kept in the top of that barn to be fed to the horse, but in the early thirties the car was kept in the lower area and the upper area was used to store junk, and for us children to play in whenever it rained.

It was easier to maintain a horse than a car. In winter, the water had to be drained from the radiator. Before the car could be used again, the radiator had to be filled with water and then the engine cranked to get it started. In those days, a person could break an arm from the backlash of the car crank. The main door to that barn was made of two parts. In former days, when the horse was kept there the upper half remained open.

Heights were always a problem for me, especially when my brother Joe threatened to throw me out of the window. In 1948, shortly after my entrance into the monastery, construction on the new monastery building was stopped due to a lack of funds. It was resumed in late 1952, and I was assigned to the building crew. As the building went up, so did the scaffolding, and I had to overcome my fear of heights. In time, I was working on the roof, helping with the slate. After that, it was the bell tower.

Father, now that I have passed my seventy-sixth year I feel as though I am nearing the top of the ladder and soon will step into the world above to be able to play with my big brothers, the saints, who have gone on ahead of me.

4 : 3 0   A M

(G e n e s i s   2 9 : 2 0) "To win Rachel, therefore, Jacob worked seven years, and they seemed to him like a few days because he loved her so much." When I was a young monk, this text—and the length of Jacob's commitment—impressed me very much. Now that I am growing older, seven years seems like a very short time, and yet the major changes of life seem to come about every seven years: 7 - 14 - 21 - 28 - 35 - 42 - 49 - 56 - 63 - 70. *What is time to You, O God? In Your eternal* Now *You see all. When Your Son Jesus walked this earth, He knew the limitations of space and time, but now He transcends all of this.*

You are now with me in the center of my being, and with the eyes of faith I behold the light that enlightens the darkness of this night, symbolized by this banana room. Seven years! Where will I be seven years from now? How far away that seems and yet how near. If love for You fills my heart, it will go quickly. Will I be with You in eternity or will I still be waiting in time? What difference does it make as long as love brings me closer to You?

4 : 3 0   A M

I am sitting in the light, but You, God, are still a hidden God. Where can I flee from Your sight? Your light illumines everything even as You seem to stay in the shadows. When will I see You as You now see me? Faith gives me the vision to see into this night and You are here. I see You now only with the eyes of faith.

(G e n e s i s   3 2)   Jacob is journeying back to his homeland, and he is "greatly afraid and distressed." What will he encounter with his brother Esau? Should he be afraid, or will his brother embrace him with love? *This journey reminds me of my own journey as I approach You, Father.* Jacob said to Esau, "'I came into your presence as into the presence of God, but you have received me kindly.'" *For me, to be journeying home to You is like venturing into the unknown. As I draw nearer to You, I hold fast to those things I treasure. Who is the Rachel in my life? Who is the Joseph in my life? Why should I fear as I come closer to You? Questions, questions, questions in the night. I wrestle with Your presence, and yet You come to me in the guise of Esau, my brother.*

St. Benedict says in his Rule for monks that I should run to You with an enlarged heart, as fear gives way to love. Yet, in reality, I find myself limping like Jacob, as I come closer to You.

As a monk, I come to You with no wives or children (according to the flesh), but You have blessed me with many "spiritual children." I have no livestock or property, except for the junk that I have accumulated in my room: old class notes, journals, photos, a passport, carvings from Africa, old letters, etc. Still, someday I must walk away from all of this to come to You. What have I to fear as I limp into the darkness of the unknown in order to come to You? And yet, You are here with me as I write!

4:30 AM

(Genesis 35) *Father, You are a God who seems to manifest Yourself most clearly in times of transition. At least this is what seems to be revealed of You in Genesis. Whenever You do manifest Yourself, it becomes a time for building a memorial to recall the event. Normally, You seem to let things happen as You silently stand by and watch.*

You are a God of silence. You manifest yourself whenever You want us to move on. Why is this? Is this a time of transition or a time of rest? You are silent, and yet You speak to me through my forefathers. You spoke to Adam, Noah, Abraham, Isaac, and now Jacob. You speak to me as You spoke to them.

What is Your message? What are You saying to me today? Why don't You speak more clearly? I think I am listening as I wait.

4:30 AM

(Genesis 37) *You, Father, are a God of history. You know everything before it happens, for You see all in Your timeless, eternal* Now. "Joseph was seventeen years old" *and you gave him dreams of what he would become. When I was seventeen, could You see me as I now write to You in this Abbey church?*

You looked down upon our fathers Abraham, Isaac, Jacob, and Joseph. You now look down on me. You know who I am and from where I have come. You saw me as a child riding on the back of that White truck with Baby Joe. You saw me on the night of my senior prom alone with Marilyn under a sky filled with stars. You saw me as a novice as I picked those half-ripe, small tomatoes. You saw me as I waved to the black children as we rode by the tenant houses of this monastery property. You saw me while I took part in the building of this monastery. You saw me as I helped Brother Felix build forms for these walls, forms which held concrete, poured wheelbarrow after wheelbarrow, in order to make the monastery walls. You saw me as I handed the slate to Fred Voight as the roof was being covered.

Through all of these experiences, You gave me the knowledge to supervise and construct the church for the sisters at Abakaliki, Nigeria. You saw me building that round altar of black volcanic stone to You. And, You see me now as I write to the sound of rain falling on the slate roof of this church. Who are You who saw Abraham, Isaac, Jacob, and Joseph, and now me? I hear You say through the Scriptures, "I Am who I Am."

This cellar, even with the lights on, symbolizes the very depth of my being in You. It is where You are a hidden God of light, and You are here.

4 : 3 0   A M

(G e n e s i s   4 5)   has just been read to us. With tears in my eyes, I recall Pope John XXIII saying to some Jewish visitors to the Vatican: "I am your brother, Joseph." When will that day arrive when Christians and Jews will recognize each other as brothers and sisters? When will older brothers come to the banana room to release their younger brothers? When will brothers embrace each other and eat together at the table of the Lord? When, when, when?

Not only are we brothers, but "we together are Christ's Body." Jesus depends on us to take that flour and make unleavened bread and say: "This is My Body." To take the wine and say: "This is My Blood shed for love of you." Love is the answer. "'This is my commandment: love one another, as I have loved you.'"

4 : 3 0   A M

(E x o d u s   3)   *Father, You have asked me to turn on the lights and to pray to You from another perspective. I am reminded of my visit to Mount Sinai in 1980. Of all the people who flew in from Israel to visit that holy mount on that day, I was the only one privileged to venerate the spot where You appeared to Moses at the burning bush. It was there that You promised to be with Moses. You are now with me on my journey through the desert of life and approach the promised land.*

Sinai from the air seemed to be so desolate. Why would anyone want to fight a war over that land of sand? *Why should a nation march through that wilderness unless You are with them? Father, send to us another Moses to lead us to You. A*

*Moses that will bring all Christians to live as brothers and sisters
and thus to establish Your kingdom upon this earth.*

Psalm 103 speaks in a special way of You.

He satisfies my desires with good things,
so that my youth is renewed like the eagle's.

He made known his ways to Moses,
his deeds to the people of Israel:

The LORD is compassionate and gracious, slow to anger,
abounding in love.

He will not always accuse, . . .

He does not treat us as our sins deserve.

As a father has compassion on his children,
so the LORD has compassion on those who fear him;
for he knows how we are formed,
he remembers that we are dust.

4:30 AM

*In   Exodus   You spoke to Moses and gave him three
signs whereby others would know that You spoke to him: power
over creatures, power over sickness, power over the elements of
nature. How often do You speak as clearly to human beings as
You spoke with Moses? It happens rarely, or does it?*

*In the Scriptures, I behold You speaking to Abraham, to Isaac,
to Jacob, and to Moses. Are You now speaking to me in the darkness of this church? What are you saying? All I am able to hear
is the silence of this night. I simply sit here in this silence and
wait.* "Speak, [Lord], for your servant is listening."

4 : 3 0   A M

Archeologists and others have dug around our monastery property and have found points made by Native Americans 10,000 years ago. This land is filled with relics of the past, of Native Americans who lived here hundreds and thousands of years ago. I recall the Sunday afternoons when I walked the fields around the monastery and found arrow points and potsherds. We now have more than 1,000 arrow points in our collection.

The Book of Hebrews begins by telling us that "At various times in the past and in various different ways, God spoke to our ancestrors through the prophets, but in our own time, the last days, he has spoken to us through his Son," Jesus. I'm listening.

The ten plagues of Egypt have taken place and now, at last, You lead Your people toward the desert. You go before them with a cloud by day and a pillar of fire by night. Within this cloud, within this pillar of fire, we are secure and safe, for You are with us, and yet we murmur. You lead us, not by the short way, but by the long way. You destroy our enemies as we are on the march. What does all this mean to me?

I simply sit in this Abbey church and wait. Your light is a pillar of fire to me as I wait. I pray in this light and yet it is night.

4 : 3 0   A M

(E x o d u s   1 4)   You tell Your people, "'Stand firm, and you will see what Yahweh will do to save you today: the Egyptians you see today, you will never see again. Yahweh will do the fighting for you: you have only to keep still.'" You ask them to be still, and yet You ask them to go through the sea. You ask us to "'Be still, and know that I am God.'" Here I am in the stillness of this night waiting for Your victory.

In our age we saw Your victory as you tore down the Berlin Wall. But we have also seen very uncertain times and many new walls. There are walls that only You can tear down: Walls that divide Christians, walls of sin and hatred, the walls between the rich and the poor. Walls, walls, walls! The walls of the sea came down to destroy the army of the enemy. The walls that divide us from You must also come down. With faith we penetrate those walls. There You are, the Father of Love.

PRAYING IN THE LIGHT OF PILGRIMAGE

5 : 1 5   A M

H e r e   I   s i t ,   praying in Your light, but far away from my home. I sit in the silence of another abbey church, in the Abbey of La Trappe, France. I am here on a pilgrimage for the celebration of the 900th anniversary of the foundation of Citeaux, the motherhouse of our Cistercian Order.

Here I sit in darkness, waiting for a new day to be born, waiting for Your light. Here I rest in Your presence, Father. Here in Your presence I bask in the peace of Your abiding love.

I thank You for the grace of visiting the cellar of the house in which St. Thérèse of Lisieux was born. I have seen the cellar in which little Thérèse would rather spend the night than say yes to her mother. I had to stoop down in order to enter into that sacred space, a low room in which potatoes are beginning to sprout. With these new memories I go down into my own cellar to close and lock the door in order to pray to You, Father, the Father who sees all that takes place even in secret.

5 : 1 5   A M

H e r e   I   a m   at La Trappe, France, while in Georgia my brothers are just now going to bed. No longer do I find here the severe monastic life as it was once lived by Jean-Armand de Rancè, a great reformer of the Cistercian order during the seventeenth century. Thomas Merton refers to that time period at La Trappe as the days of "the suicide squad." The average monk died within five years of joining, and before the age of forty. Today, I find a community of monks, some of whom are old. I find a community that is vibrant in its own unique way. Some of these monks look back longing for the good old days, while others look to the future.

Today, we leave to go on to our grandmother house of Melleray. I wish it were possible to spend more time here to ponder, reflect, and pray on the La Trappe of yesterday, today, and tomorrow. Time to ponder on the Spirit that led de Rancè, Augustin de Lestrange, and the Spirit that is leading this community today. *Here I pray to You, Father, on this soil filled with a history unique to itself.*

6 : 3 0   A M

H e r e   a t   M e l l e r a y ,   our grandmother house in northwest France, I pray before You, Father, in this Abbey church that is over 850 years old. This community of monks now numbers about twenty-one, but at one time there were more than two hundred monks here. In silence I come before You to praise You for the present moment and, with hope, to walk into the future. While travelling around France, seeing some of the sights and experiencing some of what pilgrims have experienced in this ancient land for millenia, I miss the early morning, 4:30 AM times of prayer at my own monastery in Georgia. We can enter into the cellar and close and lock the door—turning on the lights—wherever we are. But still, we sometimes yearn for that special place.

4 : 3 0   A M

Father, You have brought me to this Monastery of Tamié here in the French Alps. This is, beyond a doubt, the most beautiful monastery in the world, lost in the midst of these snow-capped peaks. This Abbey, dating back to the twelfth century, is in a small valley fed by a bubbling mountain stream.

Yesterday, You brought Jeanne and Elizabeth, two of our Lay Cistercians, and me to this paradise on earth. The hospitality of the monks, their singing, and the surroundings all serve to bring us closer to You, Father.

Even here the monks take a break between the first and second nocturn of vigils. This gives to me the silence needed to rest in Your presence, and yet, I ponder on the sufferings of the members of Your Son's body, the Church. It is only through suffering that we enter into glory, a glory reflected in the grandeur of these Alps. These, too, are aspects of Your light.

J u s t   t o   b e h o l d   the beauty that now surrounds me is in itself a prayer. There are indeed times when I need to descend into the cellar, but for now, I just stand in awe at the grandeur of these French Alps. *To You, Father, be praise through Your Son Jesus in the Holy Spirit. Amen.*

4 : 3 0   A M

Here I rest in Your presence back in the corner of the Abbey church in Conyers. Thank You for the grace of going to the 900th anniversary of the founding of Citeaux, the Motherhouse of the Cistercian Order. Thank You for the grace of being the chaplain for the Lay Cistercians of this house. Now I can rest in Your presence to recall the visits to Citeaux, La Trappe, Melleray, Laval, Tamié, and Sept-Fons.

There were also visits to the sites of Fontenay, built in the twelfth century and now owned by a private family; Molesme, also owned privately by another family; and Clairvaux, now a prison. There were the visits to Lisieux and all the places that little Thérèse wrote about in her autobiography, *Story of a Soul.* There was the house in which she was born with its cellar; the house in which she grew up; the churches in which she prayed; and the convent in which she lived and died. She was close to us all.

During the trip, I saw St. Thérèse in my mind's eye as the engineer at the front of a train. Her head was sticking out of the window of the locomotive and her long hair was blowing in the wind as in the play where she took the part of St. Joan of Arc. I became aware that she was taking charge of our journey during this pilgrimage.

There was Rue de Bac with the remains of St. Catherine; the body of St. Vincent de Paul and his big nose; the city of Nevers with the body of St. Bernadette; Paray Le Monial with St. Margaret Mary and her encounters with the Sacred Heart. *All of this I recall as I sit in this corner of the Abbey church to give praise to You, Father.*

4 : 3 0   A M

Y e s t e r d a y ,   *Jacki read over my notes to You, Father, penned during our pilgrimage to France. She was surprised that I wrote so little about the main purpose of our trip.*

Perhaps this is due to my not spending time in silent prayer before You in the early hours of the morning while at Citeaux. Then again, how does one put into words the graces that come from praying before the relics of our founding father, St. Robert of Molesme? There I was before that 900-year-old skull and bones that once held the dynamic spirit of a man of ideals. How does one express in words a gathering of 750 brothers and sisters of the Cistercian family within the newly constructed Abbey Church of Citeaux? How does one say "Thank You" for sending me to that marvelous place?

Sometimes Your light makes the words of prayer unnecessary. The places where we try to pray to You sometimes move us to be silent. More and more, I am realizing that silence is the best response to encountering You in the light.

4 : 3 0   A M

S e v e n   y e a r s   a g o ,   after the Easter Vigil Service, I went to my room to look over some of the personal belongings of my sister, Catherine, which had just been sent to me by her superior. (My sister was Sr. Catherine; she entered the Apostles of the Sacred Heart in 1938.) To my surprise I discovered some letters I had sent to Catherine fifty years earlier. One of them was about meditation.

A L L   S O U L S   D A Y ,   *1 9 4 8* .
Meditation. We have forty-five minutes of meditation each day, fifteen minutes before collation (a light supper) and the rest takes place in the cold, dreary, Georgia night. On an average day that is between 2:30 and 3 AM; on Sundays, 2 to 2:30 AM; and on big feast days, 1:30 to 2 AM. When I was at college I found seven hours of sleep to be plenty, but here I need seven hours plus the time of meditation. During that long half hour I've tried about everything to stay awake. I've moved my fingers and toes, pinched myself, stood up for a short while and then knelt again. Constantly my eyes are on the clock in the front of the chapel, but I am always half asleep. This week I started to use the book *Preparation for Death* by St. Alphonse. I have found the book to be very help- ful in helping me stay awake. If I fall asleep, the book falls to the floor and the noise wakes me up. Yes, it is very simple to talk to Jesus in the daytime, but during the early hours it is a different story.

Here I am more than fifty years later still praying to You, Father, in the early hours of the morning, but now it is between 4:30 and 5 AM. Thanks for making this aspect of our life easier than it used to be!

4 : 3 0   A M

No longer do I go down into the cellar to pray to You, Father.
Now, I simply wait in the light of Your presence.

O n   T u e s d a y ,   twenty-three Presbyterian
ministers who are here on retreat took turns reading my
reflections on *Praying in the Cellar.* Yesterday evening we
read together the parts where I exposed my fears of
darkness, of strangers, of sexuality, and of growing old and
falling apart. Afterwards one of the ministers shared with
me that I have many children, though not according to the
flesh. *Yes! There are my Ibo children in Nigeria, Lay
Cistercians associated with this monastery, and even these
Presbyterian ministers, who, although they have much to teach
me, I also teach them and together we are Your children.* Author
Frank Bianco in his book *Voices of Silence,* writes of a
Trappist brother at the Abbey of Gethsemani in Kentucky
who always dreamed of having a family of his own.
Despite his vows in the monastery, he continued to wonder
if God wanted him to love a wife and children. So, he left
the monastery and went to live with his brother, and his
wife and children, in order to better listen to what God
wanted with his life. After some months of facing the
realities of married life, he decided to return to the cloister.

Yesterday, on the table in the reading room, I came
across a book I have been looking for, *The Cloister Walk* by
Kathleen Norris, where she writes about the peace of the
monastic life. She is not a Catholic, and yet she sees the
balance and rhythm of this life. Her writing, too, helped
me to again know for certain: I am where God wants me
to be—that I know. *I pray now, Father, for You to manifest
Your love and peace to these ministers now praying with us in the*

darkness and silence of this night. Let them also pray to You in the fullness of Your light.

4:30 AM

What does it mean to be chosen by You, God? Yesterday at the Lay Cistercian meeting Dom Armand, our fourth abbot, reminded us that 900 years ago, in 1098, St. Robert was chosen at the age of seventy to lead our fathers out of Molesme to Citeaux.

In Acts chapter seven, St. Stephen reminded us that Moses was chosen at the age of eighty to lead Your people out of Egypt, and yet "'It was the same Moses that they had disowned when they said, 'Who appointed you to be our leader and judge?'" *Here I am, nearing eighty years old myself, and You have chosen me to be who I am, just as You have chosen each individual who lives. There You are, a Trinity of Love and Light, dwelling within each conscience, each heart, within each cellar. You dwell with us as a God of Love. You are hidden in each human heart. This is one of the most important teachings of Vatican II—on the human conscience as the dwelling place of Your Being—and it needs to be proclaimed to the world.*

You have called me to be Your son and so like Jesus, I am able to call you Abba, Father. *You have called me to do Your will, to give my* fiat, *to say my yes to all that is happening in my life, even as I approach death I am no longer able to hear the alarm of my watch. Yesterday it went off at 12 noon during the consecration of the community Mass and it disturbed Br. Juan Diego. Others also must have heard it, but I am deaf to that frequency. Fiat. May Your will be done on earth and also within the cellar of my heart.*

PRAYING IN THE LIGHT OF DREAMS

4:30 AM

What does it mean that Stephen "gazed into heaven and saw the glory of God, and Jesus standing at God's right hand," as described in Acts 7 as read at the first nocturn? *Do we need martyrs to die for You today? Is the blood of martyrs still needed in order to bring about the conversion of sinners?*

I pray that I will not be so oblivious to Your presence that You'll need to do the same to me. Let me see in Your light.

I had a very strange dream last night. I was driving a car that only went in reverse, and I could not stop it. For some reason, I realized that there were only two things that could be done: drive the car until it ran out of gas, or somehow add water to the tank to make it stop. Am I going backwards? How do I stop this car?

Yesterday, I stood behind Dom Augustine, our retired third abbot, as the therapist was once again slowly helping him learn to walk again. This great former leader is now recovering from a stroke. *As he slowly goes along in time, is he running to Your eternal embrace? So many detours, so many endings, even though we are in Your Light, Father.*

4:30 AM

I had another strange dream. We were preparing for an apparition of Mary in my home town of Avonmore, Pennsylvania. She was to appear at two different sites: one near the Swartz farm and the other near the Heinz factory. This was my first time to be present at an apparition. Dom Armand was with me, and he pointed out some large blackberries which we picked and ate.

The apparition site was a large field and at that point in the dream I began sincerely hoping that I would not wake up until it was finished.

I stood in a large room and just outside the window a row of the VIPs sat waiting for the apparition to happen. Brother Mark, our prior, was one of them. There were very few others present. At that moment, I somehow sensed that the sun would become dim and that Mary would appear visibly as a bright object. Only a few of her features would be visible, and only to those who stood or sat up front. Then, as suddenly as it began, the dream ended. What does it mean? Why am I inside and not outside? *What does this have to do with my wanting to pray to You, Lord, in the light?*

4 : 3 0   A M

I s   i t   t h e   p r o p h e t   Joel that says the young will see visions and the old will dream dreams? The other night I had a dream in which I was speaking before a large audience. I told the people how I had known Dorothy Day and Thomas Merton. I spoke with Merton only a few months before his death. They too were dreamers and yet they had to face the realities of life. There is both a positive sense and a negative sense of being "a dreamer," isn't there?

(Acts 10) At this early hour I ponder on the vision given to Peter. What is this vision about—a sheet coming down from heaven containing a zoo? He is told, "'Now, Peter, kill and eat!'" These animals symbolize all the peoples of the earth who have to be cleansed by baptism, a type of death, and then to be consumed by the food they eat, the Eucharist. The dream made Peter's vocation very clear to him. *My dreams are not as clear to me, but I know that You are speaking to me through them nevertheless.*

Does Pope John Paul II also receive visions like the first pope? Does the Holy Spirit speak to him as he did to Peter? Rarely does the Holy Spirit speak in Scripture, and then only briefly. He simply indicates a direction to be taken and then leaves the rest up to the listener. The Book of Acts is filled with actions that are a response to the invitations of the Holy Spirit.

As I sit in this Abbey church, no visions come to me except the one described in the reading from Acts. I hear no words from Your Holy Spirit. I sit in Your presence, Father, and wait.

4 : 3 0   A M

We   a l l   h a v e   d r e a m s ,   don't we? Are they useless chatter in our minds or do they have something to tell us about ourselves, about God?

Dreams are a place where we can encounter the best and the worst in us. In dreams, we encounter those who have passed on to the next world, yet in dreams they still remain here with us. Dreams are indeed a part of God's creation, and it is up to us to discover the true meaning of them. The Bible says that old men will dream dreams, and it seems that I am doing more of that all of the time.

Last night there was a thunderstorm. At this early hour there is freshness in the air, and peace reigns as I sit in this corner of the Abbey church and continue to ponder on the vision of Peter. Peter had told Cornelius that he is no longer to consider unclean that which God has cleansed. Perhaps I should begin to keep a dream journal, because they are coming more frequently, now. This year, while attending a conference at Mepkin Abbey near Moncks Corner, South Carolina, I visited in the home of some friends nearby. Helen, my hostess, told me one day that whenever she invites a priest to stay in their home he usually has a special dream. It didn't happen to me and so I told Helen as I left. She said simply, "Wait."

That night, back at the abbey, a special dream came to me. I saw the elevator door of the abbey opening before me and inside the elevator—which was recently built as an aid to our aging population of monks—stood the crucified Jesus of the Passion according to Mel Gibson. There He was with all of His wounds, crowned with thorns, but holding a walker rather than carrying a cross. At that moment the dream ended. I became profoundly moved and aware that Jesus was identifying with the infirm of our community.

4 : 3 0   A M

Today I had another dream to ponder: Two dogs were injuring a third, larger, black dog. Bees were swarming and we all ran for cover. This dream reminds me again of the vision of Peter and the zoo coming down in a tarpaulin. It also reminds me of a time, about 1961, when Fr. Michael asked me to drive him to an abandoned house that had bees in the outer wall. I put on a mask, and he handed me a smoke pot that had to be pumped like an accordion. While he tore down the inner wall to get to the honeycomb, I stood by, smoking the bees away. In spite of the protective garb, the bees were stinging me through my clothing. I was drenched in sweat. As we drove back to the monastery I began to get sick. I went at once to Fr. Cyprian, the infirmarian, and told him that I probably had heat stroke, and then said, "Incidentally, I have been stung by about fifty bees." He put me to bed at once and called a doctor. As the Ibo saying goes: "I survived the night."

Once we have faced our fears in the dark cellar, we emerge stronger and more joyful. But now, even as I pray to You, Father, in Your light, the dreams that You send to me are sometimes not only confusing, but give rise again to my fears.

4 : 3 0   A M

At this time of the morning I am able to recall the past, be aware of the present, or dream of the future. Before rising on this particular morning, I had a dream of a future monastery I would visit. It was the Conyers community and the buildings were also large. The church was full of monks and at times I was in deep prayer. Outside, someone with a truck gave me a ride. We traveled over the fields and arrived at a large sea. Returning later to the abbey, I heard from without the voices of many monks singing the *Salve*. Then, on seeing the simplicity of the living quarters I was moved to tears. I was trying to tell one of the monks that I was from the past, but he seemed not to comprehend this.

In the next dream, I was at a future Mass. I recognized the man who was the deacon. He and the celebrant had very ornate vestments and mitered hats much like those used in the oriental churches. The altar was set high up on steps. Much incense was used and when they finished with the incense, it was put into a tabernacle called an incense house. The door of the tabernacle was left slightly open, and the smoke of the incense kept rolling out.

As children came from the side, and the celebrant gave them the Eucharist, saying, "Become the Body of Christ," I looked over to see my deceased brother Joe who was seated at my side.

I am able to recall the past, be present in the now of time, but dream of the future. . . .

4 : 3 0   A M

T h e   B o o k   o f   A c t s   (chapter 12) reveals the power of angels. Where are these angels of light today? Why was Peter freed, while on the other hand James was beheaded? Is the intervention of angels so rare that when it does happen it is written in the Scriptures? Or, is the opposite nearer to the truth?

Perhaps we are being reminded of the nearness of angels and of their reality? I have never seen an angel. Or, have I? Some years back, a bearded stranger walked into our guesthouse and spoke to me while I was working in the office. He said, "The Father is pleased with this place." I answered that the Father is pleased with many places, but he insisted that the Father was pleased with this place. I then asked, "Where are you from?" He answered, "I am from near, and I am from afar." Then, he repeated those words once more. I asked him if he wanted to stay for supper, but as I looked up I noticed that he had already left. I was not sure if he heard me, so I got up from behind the desk and went to the door, but no one was there. Was he an angel?

Perhaps I have not recognized angels in human disguise. The early church thought Peter was an angel. We live in a world of mysteries. *We see so much when we stand in Your light. But, what is it that we do not yet see?*

4 : 3 0 A M

(A c t s   1 3)   We behold the early church being born among the nations with the preaching of forgiveness of sins and the promise of eternal salvation. But this message has yet to be proclaimed to the ends of the earth.

I am reminded of how this message was brought to Dismas of Calabar as he waited on death row in a stadium in Nigeria on February 23, 1987. I met Dismas of Calabar that day, as he stood before 20,000 people. There were ten prisoners set to be executed; most of them were singing and trying to dance with their shackled hands and feet, as they stood before the vast crowd.

The people shouted and sang at this strange, liturgical-like celebration of death. It was much like the activity that goes on at a baseball game when the score is tied and the bases are loaded in the bottom of the ninth inning. These men were about to be publicly executed, and here they were dancing and singing along with 20,000 people.

As I watched this strange drama, one of the prisoners looked up at me and our eyes caught each other. I, in my monastic garb, and he in his prison garb; our eyes caught in an embrace of understanding. I raised my hand and gave him a blessing. He, in turn, took his shackled hands and signed himself with the sign of the cross. I knew he was Catholic.

Our silent conversation ended as he was taken across to the other side of the stadium and tied to a post. The military chaplains, one Protestant and the other Catholic, went to each of the ten prisoners and spoke words of comfort and forgiveness.

After that, seven military men marched to the center of the field and orders were shouted out: "Get on your knees! Aim! Fire!" Then came the sound of those automatic rifles followed by dead silence! I watched my newfound friend as he turned aside and then went limp. All ten prisoners were shattered with bullet wounds. At that point, the physician crossed the field and indicated that not all of the men were dead. Again, the order was called out: "Get on your knees! Aim! Fire!"

Will I ever forget that moment in time? Not a chance. The barrier on the side of the stadium came down as people rushed out onto the field. An army truck then drove out to remove the bodies and the chaplain whispered into my ear, "Let's get out of here. There is going to be a riot." We were driven away in a military car.

It was only later that I learned that my new friend, Dismas, was baptized on the day that he was publicly executed. I now call upon him as Saint Dismas of Calabar. But, how do I pray after experiencing a thing like this? *Nevertheless I enter into the silence of this night, and the safety of Your shade, and I pray.*

4 : 3 0   A M

In this morning's reading from Acts 15, Peter tells us that You are able to read our minds, or as another translation puts it, You "know our hearts." Before You, Father, I come just as the early church came before You to seek Your will for me. What are You asking of me today?

You want us to celebrate. To celebrate Your goodness, Your presence in us and among us. The West does not know how to celebrate as they do in the African cultures that I have experienced. African culture seems to have a natural understanding for true, heartfelt celebration. Food makes up only a portion of the celebration, whether it be a birth, a death, or some other very special event. I have even seen jubilant celebrations of Catholic ceremonies, such as the solemn profession of a nun, whereby a young woman gives herself totally to You and to Your Son, Jesus, for the rest of her life.

Unless we learn to celebrate with music and dance we will not really be able to celebrate with You, Father, in the eternal banquet of Your Love. The nuns of Abakaliki, Nigeria, usually put on a skit for special guests. The skit is preceded by dancing and then followed by a play. I doubt if any Hollywood production could measure up to some of the performances I have seen. My favorite is that of the prodigal son. One of the nuns takes the place of the prodigal son, and whenever he is feeding the pigs, she in turn would be feeding our two German shepherd dogs. The role of the loyal son is portrayed by another nun, who walks in with produce from the farm.

These celebrations remind me of the story of St. Francis of Assisi using live animals and people to create the first real celebration of Christmas—the first nativity crèche. Francis and his early followers were known as "God's jugglers." *That is the sort of joy that we need as we also dance in Your light.*

4 : 3 0   A M

"'Y o u r   s o n s   a n d   d a u g h t e r s shall prophesy, your old men dream dreams.'" This passage from the prophet Joel again comes to mind because today it appears in the homily of St. Peter on the first Sunday of Pentecost.

The other night I had a dream, as our brothers of the Old Testament—Joseph and Daniel—had dreams. They were not old men, but mere youths, when they had their dreams. I was speaking to an audience and I said: "We are at the beginning of a new era of renewal. One of the greatest renewals ever to take place in the world is about to unfold with a new Pentecost, a new era of peace, where the peace of the Holy Spirit will reign in human hearts. We will behold wonders and dream dreams as we are about to enter into this remarkable new age." Then, the dream came abruptly to an end.

4 : 3 0   A M

L a s t   n i g h t I had my dream of all dreams. Watching a video, I saw Babi, my grandfather, kneeling with his head bowed in prayer. Next, I saw old Brother Pius and he pointed to the videoscreen that I was watching, as if to say without words, "Look!" I began to hold Babi, my grandfather, in prayer to You, Father, and then Babi said in perfect English: "Glory be to the Father, and to the Son, and to the Holy Spirit. Amen."

Is this dream my own wish fulfillment, to see my Babi again, and to know that he is in heaven with you, Lord? I do not know for sure, but I do know that in Your light, Father, I may see myself even more clearly than I did in the dark.

It is the climax of all creation and all celebration, to give praise to You, Father, Son, and Holy Spirit. Amen.

IV

Encountering God in the Shade

T h e   w o r d   *h e a r t*   appears over a thousand
times in the Bible. The biblical notion of heart is the
dwelling place where I am, and where I live. It is my hidden
center beyond even the grasp of reason. To enter into the
cellar is analogous to entering into your heart.

From the corner in the Abbey church at 4:30 AM, I have
ventured into the cellar of my youth; into that banana

room and ultimately into the very center of my being, my heart. It is in that sacred space in the center of my being, my conscience, that the Triune God lives and dwells. This is the great adventure inward: the journey from loneliness to solitude.

Up to this point, I have invited you to go with me into the cellar, the darkness of the cellar, into the light of God, and now into the shade.

Why the shade? In the Gospel of John, Jesus says to us: "I am the light of the world; anyone who follows me will not be walking in darkness; he will have the light of life." So, why would we choose to encounter God in the shade?

I recall the days when our monastery was in the cattle business. Cattle grazed in the pasture during the early hours of the day, but in the heat of the day the cows migrated to the shade of the trees to slowly digest the grass they had previously eaten. They kept chewing the cud until it was digestible. We, in turn, must withdraw from the heat of the day and retire into the shade and there ponder on that which has fed us as we grazed in the light.

There are different kinds of shade. The shade of the tree is able to shelter us from the heat of the sun, but one is also able to sit under a tree when there is a full moon and there one encounters another kind of shade.

To God, darkness and light are the same since nothing is hidden from Him, and yet like the astronomers we need to enter into the darkness of the night in order to behold the beauty of the stars. Astronomers cannot study the stars and the planets during the daytime. They must wait until it is dark to look through their telescopes and see all of the glories of the heavens. They have to work in the night in order to ponder the skies and the vastness of outer space.

Similarly, if we hunger for understanding, we must accept that the shade is often the best place to be.

We saw this darkness in the banana room, but for now we have come to enter into another experience, perhaps symbolizing another mode of prayer. In the darkness of that banana room we were unable to read for we were in total darkness. But now we are either able to read and ponder on the Scripture, or like the monks at 4:20 AM we can listen to the readings and then go to our corner of the church to ponder on the sacred text. We will do a lot of this in this chapter.

Years ago, I received a letter from a young woman after she read the first edition of *Praying in the Cellar*. The letter really touched me because I felt that she had truly grasped the essence of what I am trying to do in these teachings about contemplative prayer. She wrote:

Dear Father Anthony,

I have shed no tears since my boyfriend was laid in the ground after an eight-month struggle with cancer. I was "strong," and held his hand as he took his last breaths. At his graveside, I buried myself along with him. There would be no more tears.

Six years later, I find myself sitting in the Abbey church at 3:45 AM, alone. I have read *Praying in the Cellar* twice now, and though I am frightened to enter my inner room, I am trusting in your words: "The ability to face the fears of the past is a grace from the Father. I am called to face the reality of who I am and where I have come from."

It is now 4:30 AM. I am here in the darkened quiet of the Abbey church. In this silence I hear God beckoning—I will not be taking this walk alone. I take a deep breath and begin, at last, my journey to remember. I become my memories so that I may fully understand the person God has made me to be.

Father Anthony, your words have given me the courage and understanding to begin this journey. This monastery has become a true retreat from the world for me.

I thank God for you, your words, and wisdom which I ponder here in the silence.

I now understand that tears are okay.

In Christ's love, Jennifer

Like Jennifer, each of us in turn must face those fears that haunt us. Like her, we must face the reality of who we are. This is the essence of what I have been saying in the first three chapters of this book. We have to make our prayer—our encounters with God—personal, and we also need to listen to the Scriptures as they speak a personal message to you and to me.

Journaling will help us process those fears. Follow with me as I journal my encounters with the Father and with the past. One of my friends kept a journal for years, but she was later afraid to re-read what was written there. These journals needed to be re-read, but in the presence of the Father who heals all. Only God is able to extend to us the mercy we need to face all of those blunders of the past.

The idea of encountering God in the shade is surely a new concept for most people. Why would we move from praying in the light—God's light—to pray in the shade? The shade implies that the sun is shining and that I am outside resting under a tree. God finds us in the darkness, but as St. John of the Cross says, such darkness is "a light too bright for our eyes." We see through things—through Scripture, through our experiences, through other people. Revelation is not yet complete. Rest in the shade, and the Father will find you and speak with you there. That is what is best for you, now.

This last series of meditations represents another transition in contemplative prayer. Here, we pass from reflecting on our past experiences and begin to be more absorbed with the present. Listen and the Spirit will lead you along on this process.

I am reflecting on the latter section of the Book of Acts throughout these meditations. Again, I suggest that you have your Bible handy, and read along with us in the Abbey. Then, come with me to the corner of the church and together let us ponder on their meanings in our lives.

4 : 3 0   A M

B e f o r e   Y o u ,   F a t h e r , *I begin to pray and listen in the shade of this night.* What is night but the shade of the world, since the sun is shining on the other side of the globe? The sun is shining on another part of this earth, and here I am at 4:30 AM in the shade of this world in this night.

Instead of my imagination taking me into the cellar of my youth, I simply sit in the shade of this night in Your presence, Father, and wait. But what am I waiting for?

I will wait for the dawn. We have made artificial dawns simply by flicking on the switch and beholding day instead of night. But maybe there is a reason why You asked me to turn off the lights.

I sit in the darkness of this Abbey, scribbling under the light that shines dimly way up over the door leading into the guesthouse. I cannot even read what I am writing. The Paschal candle is burning before me as a sign that this is the Easter season, and that Your Son Jesus has risen from the dead, but He has not truly risen until all the members of His Body have risen with Him. As long as my brothers remain in the cemetery just outside that door, Jesus has not fully risen in the totality of His Body, the Church.

A light shines on the tabernacle and a candle burns before it as a sign that Jesus is truly and Eucharistically present, that Jesus is here with me in the shade of this night.

The louvered exhaust fans in the roof are blowing to keep the Abbey church cool on this warm May night. The noise of the fans again muffle the sound of noise caused by my writing on this paper. The monks praying around me are not disturbed by my scribbling.

The Scripture reading for the first nocturn comes from Acts 16. The Holy Spirit tells Paul "'. . . not to preach the word in Asia.'" The Spirit instead opened other doors including the heart of a woman called Lydia. *Is Your Spirit also leading the Church of today? You open doors for us to freely enter in, and then You seem to stand by and wait for us to do our part in bringing the world into the heart of Your Son, Jesus Christ. What will this new dawn, this new day, bring into my life? What doors will Your Spirit open for me today?*

4 : 3 0   A M

(A c t s   1 6)   St. Paul casts out the evil spirit of fortune-telling from a slave girl. As a result they are imprisoned. "Late that night Paul and Silas were praying and singing God's praises, . . ." *Is the middle of the night not the best time to pray to You, Father?* I think so! Here in the shade of this night, I wait for the true dawn. It is here before you that I am cleansed and refreshed to face the coming of a new day.

4 : 3 0   A M

(A c t s   1 7) *In the shade of this world, this night, I continue my journey with Paul and Silas. I hear no messages from You, Father, neither do I see visions, but I do dream dreams.*

Last night in my dream I saw a wild lion on the other side of a fence. On my side I was with a tame black tiger. The tiger forced itself through the fence, and the lion attacked it. A great struggle took place between the two of them. Then I saw the four black cubs of the tiger also attacking the lion. I was helpless as I looked on from my side of the fence. Both the lion and the black tiger were killed, but the four cubs were safe. I realized that the black tiger went through the fence in order to save her children. What is the significance of this dream? Who was the lion? Who was the tame black tiger? Who were the four cubs? Why death? *I can ask the questions, but I need not answer them; they will rest in You.*

4 : 3 0   A M

(A c t s   1 7) This morning I find myself with Paul in Athens. He is in shock to behold this great city worshipping idols. What, I wonder, would Paul say if he were visiting the world of today? What would he say about our educational system, our myopia with science, our consumerism, our violence, our media, our poverty? What would Paul preach about today if he were to stand before Congress or the United Nations? "'[God] is not far from any of us, since it is in him that we live, and move, and exist. . . .'" *He tells the Athenians and me that I live, move, and have my being in You, Father. You made all that was and is and is to come. You wait patiently for us to recognize ourselves in the center of Your Being. Here I am, in Your shade, waiting for the dawn.*

4 : 3 0   A M

A s c e n s i o n   T h u r s d a y .   *Jesus has ascended to You, Father, and yet You are here with me in the shade of this night.* He has left a work for us to do until He returns. We are to proclaim the message of truth that Jesus has risen and will return again. He will return just as He left us. But, what does this mean? For almost 2,000 years we have awaited Christ's return. When He does return, what will happen? These are questions being asked from the shade of this night as we await the dawn.

In the silence of this night I hear a small electric fan blowing somewhere in the Abbey church. I also hear the ringing in my own ears caused forty years ago by a drive-it gun I used to shoot bolts into the concrete of the cloister garden. My ears are still ringing.

A small candle burns before a reliquary filled with pieces of bones from people we now call saints. Where are they now on this Ascension Thursday? They are now with You, yet a part of their mortal bodies continues to remain with us within this reliquary. What about those buried in our cemetery just outside that door?

They are now with You, Father, on this Ascension Thursday, and yet we all await that day when we also will ascend with Jesus to You.

4 : 3 0   A M

(A c t s   1 8)   *In this morning's reading, Father, we hear Your Son speak to Paul and say,* "'Do not be afraid to speak out, nor allow yourself to be silenced: I am with you.'" If God is with us, what do we have to fear? How consoling these words are!

It is not very often that You spoke to Paul, perhaps once every few years, yet the few words seem to have been enough to keep him going. You simply stepped back to see what would happen. Does this also hold true today in our relationship with You? I am here listening for those very few words.

Dreams are like building in the present moment from the stones of the past, much like the walls of the medieval Cistercian monasteries I saw while traveling in France. Those builders simply took rubble, stones, and mortar, put them together and built walls. Who is this builder in my dreams who takes events of my life that are scattered all over the place and then begins to build stories? *Are You, Father, the primary source of these dreams?*

I once had a dream that an archeologist discovered that the barn which once served as the first church on our abbey property was built onto a part of another building that dated back to the fifteenth century. I must value tradition! I realized in the dream that the older structure was a stone chimney, and upon waking, I remembered learning about a cathedral in France that was built in stages, the oldest corner going back to the eleventh century.

At times when I have been walking through the woods on this monastery property, I have come across a chimney of an old house. Chimneys are perhaps the most solidly constructed portion of a house. Yesterday, Sr. Nettie of Mississippi Abbey and I were walking in the old garden area looking for Indian artifacts. We found flakings dating perhaps from thousands of years ago.

Where do dreams come from? What is the meaning of my dream of last night? Again, I can ask the questions, but I need not answer them. *Indeed, Father, I do believe that You speak to us through dreams.*

4 : 3 0   A M

S o m e   C h r i s t i a n s   talk about light as a metaphor for holiness, and darkness as a metaphor for evil. In other words, a Christian is to run to the light and to avoid the dark. The Bible actually describes light and darkness this way. "God is light; there is no darkness in him at all. If we say that we are in union with him while we are living in darkness, we are lying because we are not living the truth. But if we live our lives in the light as he is in the light, we are in union with one another, and the blood of Jesus, his Son, purifies us from all sin." Meanwhile, darkness is where God is not. Darkness hides reality while light has power. We are to seek the light and leave the darkness behind: "Send out your light and your truth; let these be my guide, to lead me to your holy mountain and to the place where you live."

Jesus says, "'I, the light, have come into the world, so that whoever believes in me need not stay in the dark any more.'" But, as we know from Creation, God did not bring light into the world until He created the universe. Until it came time for God to relate to humankind, and to fulfill His will through the human race, the universe was form-less and void, and dark. Even before light was created, God was in His own Light.

Father, I willingly meet You in the shade today.

4 : 3 0   A M

(A c t s   1 9)   St. Luke writes in this morning's reading of the foundation of the church in Ephesus, of the coming of the Holy Spirit upon a group of leaders, and of the power of the name of Jesus to overcome evil spirits.

I am reminded of the visit of Father Ede, the wonder-working priest of Nigeria, when he was escorted by the police into Abakaliki for a healing service at the cathedral. This took place in the Spring of 1987. In front of the cathedral was a pile of juju articles, things used for witch-craft. This pile of magical juju was destined to be burned by Father Ede after the Mass. There were also thousands of five-gallon blue plastic containers filled with water for him to bless. On that particular morning, I was assigned to drive one of the sisters to the market. The market was almost empty, and thus the price of bananas was very low. In fact, they were so cheap, I decided to buy a bunch on my own to experiment with slicing and drying them in our solar oven.

Many of the shops were closed and it seemed that most of the city had gathered at the cathedral for this special Mass. We got back to the monastery early, only to discover that something was still needed from the market. So, I drove back alone to Abakaliki. While driving past the cathedral, I noticed that Fr. Ede had just arrived. I decided on the spot to attend this Mass. To my surprise, I was noticed and given VIP treatment and concelebrated Mass with Fr. Ede, along with many other priests, at their outdoor altar. There must have been at least 20,000 people present. Afterwards, Fr. Ede and I exchanged words of peace, *Shalom*, before I proceeded to the market to buy what was needed. On the way back to the village I picked up some of the villagers carrying their five-gallon containers of holy water on their heads.

Many miracles occurred as a result of that Mass. The following day, Andrew, one of our workmen, told me that his mother had been cured; others of the village also claimed healings during the Mass. The greatest miracle to me, though, was the increase in everyday spirituality among the people. Many of the villagers began attending Sunday Mass regularly.

4 : 3 0   A M

(A c t s   1 9)   Demetrius and the silversmiths almost caused a riot. The people shouted, "'Great is Diana of the Ephesians!'"

This reminds me of the day Mother Margaret Mary and I went shopping for a new car in Enugu. Those were the days when cars were still available and the naira was worth more than the American dollar. Today, the American dollar equals about 125 naira.

While we were shopping, a mob began to form. There was some sort of commotion going on nearby that we knew nothing about. Soon the police came and dispersed everyone with tear gas. People began running in every direction. Some of the gas reached us, and it felt like someone had thrown hot pepper into my eyes as tears began to flow. We ran for cover.

The noise of shouting people brought to mind the baseball game that I once attended with the pastor of my hometown parish. It was my first baseball game in more than fifty years. The thumping and shouting of the crowd was a liturgy unique to itself.

We need Your light in order to see, Father. We seek Your son, Jesus Christ, the Light of all lights. A Light which is ". . . a lamp to my feet, a light to my path." *That is the light that is ours when You speak to us, and find us, where we are.* That is the path of encountering God in the shade. The mysteries of God will not be fully revealed—the lights not fully turned on—until the end of time.

4 : 3 0   A M

(A c t s   2 0)   While Paul is preaching "Eutychus who was sitting on the window-sill grew drowsy and was overcome by sleep and fell to the ground three floors below." Paul awoke him from death. Was this truly a miracle? Luke is concerned with telling us about the experience of Eutychus, but he fails to relate to us the contents of the preaching of Paul. Did others also fall asleep during that sermon? I probably would have been one of them.

Often I have had to struggle to stay awake during the homily in the early hours in the Abbey. I can stay awake for about five minutes, and then . . . *Sometimes the shade can be too relaxing for us to hear what You would have us hear, Father.* At these times, should we return to the darkness of the cellar, or to the fullness of light?

I experienced some of the same struggles at Mount Calvary in Nigeria when old Dom Mark, the superior, would preach for fifteen minutes in English and then go on for another fifteen minutes in Ibo. I understand that his process for beatification will soon begin. Indeed, he was a holy man. Was he a saint? I would say yes! Yet even with him, I had to struggle to stay awake during his overlong homilies. Eutychus, pray for us who have to struggle to stay awake even when saints are preaching!

Old Dom Mark called me "Father Udo," short for *Udochukwu*, an Ibo word meaning "The Peace of God"— not that I have peace, but that I have to struggle to have peace. That is what life is all about.

Dom Mark was not elected as first superior of Mount Calvary, and so returned to his motherhouse in the Cameroons, at Bamenda. To my surprise, he was elected abbot of that monastery in 1982, probably due to his age and the respect that Africans have for the elderly. I was present for his Abbatial Blessing.

It was years later, about 1987, that Dom Mark stopped off at Abakaliki. He was really showing his age and was becoming mentally confused. He became uncertain of his salvation. *Sometimes Father, our aging bodies and minds begin to create darkness for us that is confusing, not enlightening. What we wouldn't give for a few hours with You in the shade, at those times! All I could do was assure Dom Mark of Your mercy and love. Indeed You are a God of mercy and a Father of love.* Dom Mark was entering his dark night of the soul.

In 1998, two million people attended the beatification of Fr. Cyprian Michael Tansi at Onitsha, Nigeria. Pope John Paul II was there to proclaim this hidden saint of our

Order as blessed. Fr. Tansi was the closest friend of Dom Mark, but it is my personal belief that Dom Mark was the greater of the two.

4 : 3 0   A M

L u k e   gives us another example of a teaching of Paul in Acts 20. In his talk Paul reminds the people at Miletus of how he lived and taught. *He is eager to go on to Jerusalem to continue to do Your will, Father. From city to city Your Spirit speaks to Paul through the prophets, telling him that trials and hardship await him.* Perhaps Luke shares with us so little of the teaching of Paul, because he knows Paul is putting this into writing through his letters to the churches.

Am I eager to do your will when I know it will involve trials and hardships?

I remember how eager I was to go to Africa in 1979, knowing that hardships awaited me. In Africa, I found that even the ordinary things were different. There was the out-house (without a "Sears and Roebuck" catalogue), washing from a bucket, drinking from a bottle rather than from the faucet (all drinking water had to be boiled first and then filtered). There was the change of diet and the constant fatigue that came along with malaria. There were those mosquitoes, sand flies, snakes, and lizards. I remember Dom Mark warning me to always look around before entering a room. Indeed, I did discover snakes at the hermitage.

That hermitage was to me a shade from the tropical sun. We needed the shade on those hot summer days! *Ironically, now that I look back, I recall some of the happiest years of my life, thanks to You, Father.*

4:30 AM

These departing words of Paul in Acts 20 are moving indeed! If only it were possible to capture something like this on video. How moving it would be to see Paul with the early Christians kneeling in prayer on the seashore, and then the kissing, the embrace, and the tears of a final good-bye.

I recall leaving home more than fifty years ago: those final farewells; then the good-byes to the black children of Holy Redeemer church, and to the children of the slums. With tears in my eyes I looked upon black children playing in the streets as the train was leaving Washington, D.C., headed south to the lands where restrooms were divided between colored and white. I was going south to pray for those to whom I had just said my good-byes.

I recall the good-byes to the nuns in the Cameroons as we left to make the foundation at Abakaliki, Nigeria, and the good-byes to Africa as I returned to the States to do Your will, Father. I remember the words of Brother Chukwuemeka who said, "I will miss you as a mother hen misses her chicks." Little did I realize that one day Brother Chukwuemeka would come to Conyers to give us a helping hand. In Africa, he was one of my students and became a spiritual son in Christ. He in turn had to say his good-bye to his fellow Nigerian monks in order to come here.

The Feast of the Ascension is a Feast of good-byes as Jesus says His farewell to His followers and returns to God the Father.

What is death but a farewell to those we love, our good-bye? There was the good-bye to St. Dismas of Calabar as we said farewell without words, and to all those buried outside this door of the Abbey cemetery. *When will my final good-bye be said to this world as I come to You, Father? What joy it will be to go to You, to do Your will, to see You not with the eyes of faith, as I now do in the shade of this night, but to see You face to face in all Your Glory! No longer will it be good-bye, but welcome home!*

4:30 AM

E a r l i e r   i n   A c t s ,   Paul, who was then called Saul, was blinded by God on the road to Damascus. Luke tells us that a light from heaven flashed about Saul on his way to Damascus to persecute Christians. "He fell to the ground, and then he heard a voice saying, 'Saul, Saul, why are you persecuting me?'" For three days, Saul lost his sight; *You took his sight from him, Father.* It wasn't until Ananias—sent by God, told by God in a vision— went to see Saul and lay hands on him that he once again could see. Not just see, but he was now filled with the Holy Spirit, Luke tells us. "Immediately it was as though scales fell away from Saul's eyes and he could see again."

Luke also tells us in Acts, chapter 13, that Saul, now baptized as Paul, rebuked a magician, saying, "'You utter fraud, you impostor, you son of the devil, you enemy of all true religion, why don't you stop twisting the straightforward ways of the Lord? Now watch how the hand of the Lord will strike you: you will be blind, and for a short time you will be unable to see the sun.'" Again, blindness!

Lead us out of the darkness, Father. Do not take our sight away from us. May I have sight and vision to know Your will for me. I am in the shade where I can see the light, where it is not too overpowering.

(Acts 21) Paul continues with a travelogue of his trip to Jerusalem. Again we find the Christian community is kneeling on the shore in prayer and saying their good-byes. Who are these prophets, both men and women who through the Spirit foresee the future? They try to persuade Paul not to go on to Jerusalem.

Even the prophets can tempt us not to do Your will, Father. Your Holy Spirit knows all that will happen and at times You reveal that future to Your prophets. Paul does not listen to them, but keeps his eyes on Jesus, Your Son, and he is willing to freely go on to Jerusalem, and even to die there, if that be Your will.

How do we discern the genuine prophets from those claiming to be a prophet? *There seems to be a lot of them coming to our guesthouse, based on the fact that so many retreatants here at the Abbey seem to have a prophetic voice in speaking to me about You and Your will. I have been told, for instance, that You want me to return to Africa to do Your will and then to die there. Others have told me that I am to remain where I am, for You have work for me to do right here. What am I to do? I simply wait for Your Spirit to manifest Your will to me through my superiors. That is the way of a monk—the voice of my abbot is as Your voice to me, and so I listen.*

If You want me to return to Africa, then You will have to open the door through my superiors. Until then, I simply wait and in this waiting Your will is being done. Here I write knowing that in Your eternal Now You see the future as present. Freely You invite me to walk into that future which is already present to You, and there to do Your will.

It was one of Your prophets who told me that You wanted me to write. At that time I thought to myself that I had nothing of importance to write, and yet I have written and continue to write in the shade of this Abbey church. I write of who I am and where

I have been. I write as honestly as I can in Your presence, Father. You know beforehand what I will write, and You see the results of this writing. You know each and every person who will ever read what is being written in the shade of this night. Nothing is hidden from You, for You are in the eternal Now. *My job and the job of every person is to freely do Your will, and to do it with love.*

4 : 3 0   A M

A f e w   y e a r s   a g o ,   while visiting our daughter house of Our Lady of the Andes in Venezuela, Brother Juan Diego took me on the highest skylift in the world. At that high altitude (13,267 feet!) I found it difficult to breathe, and I felt light-headed. It is said that the radiation from the sun increases with the altitude. Sometimes we need the shade in order to protect us from the radiation of the sun.

We can also find ourselves in the shade at night as we take shelter from the light of the moon. Last night there was a total eclipse of the moon. How that stirs my imagination! *The shade of mystery is provided by You, Father, until the day comes when we will need it no longer. I long for that day now more than ever, but now I rest in Your shade.*

I am reminded of a conference given by Jonathan Montaldo, an expert on the life and teachings of Thomas Merton, when he spoke to the monks about the short love affair Merton had with "M," a 24-year-old nurse. Merton had just turned fifty.

Romance can be short-lived. Romance is one thing, but the reality of married life is another. Merton, while in the midst of this romance, had to face the reality of seeing himself as married. He wrote to M., who was also his nurse, "If we had gotten married you would have found yourself hooked to an alcoholic ex-priest."

The world confuses love with romance. St. Paul gives us another definition of love in Corinthians 13. How many priests and monks have left to face the reality of family life with a wife and children? Only two months ago, an ex-monk told me that his heart is still in the monastery although he now has a wife and child.

Here I sit in Your presence, Father, knowing that I also had the freedom to leave and do the same. The forties and fifties can be difficult years and the choice was a difficult one. My choice was to stay. Freely did I make the choice and then to go to Africa. *Thanks to Your grace I can now look back and feel certain that I have made the right choice. Now I choose to freely walk into the future You have chosen for me. I choose freely to love You, a God who is true Love.*

4:30 AM

(A c t s 2 3) *Once again Jesus, Your Son, speaks to Paul* "'Courage! You have borne witness to me in Jerusalem, now you must do the same in Rome.'" *Paul spoke openly of Jesus before his own people, and now You are about to send him to Rome to do the same and then to die there as a martyr.*

It is only on rare occasions, Father, that You seem to have spoken to Paul, and the evangelist Luke made sure to record them. I sense in Scripture that You usually spoke when it was time for someone to move on and then You withdrew into Your silence to wait. Is that what you still do today?

Yesterday, two nurses and a doctor were here to check out the monks for prostate cancer. Thus far I am still in the running since the doctor found some abnormality in me. *What does Your future have in store?*

I am going through the belongings in my room and now have a large pile of things to be burned. Some of these are old prophecies by "prophets" about things that never materialized. Either I must throw out a lot of these notes that have accumulated, or someone else will have to do it after my death, as Dom Bernard did with the belongings of Fr. Stan. My turn cannot be far off. Even if I live seven years or seventeen years, that is a short time in respect to your eternal *Now*. All I have to do is to trust and wait.

4 : 3 0   A M

W h o   i s   t h i s   unnamed nephew who saves the life of Paul as Luke tells us in Acts 23? What of Paul's unnamed sister? I will one day be able to meet them to learn more of the details of their lives. How long was it before those who had vowed not to eat until Paul was killed had their next meal? Did any of them die of starvation? I doubt it!

In Acts 24, Paul speaks out in his own defense and does a good job of it. He could rightly say, "'I . . . do my best to keep a clear conscience at all times before God and man.'" Only You, Father, are the judge of the human conscience. You see and know who we are, and before You we stand.

Yesterday evening we had the long-awaited downpour. Thank You, Father.

4 : 3 0   A M

(A c t s   2 4)   "He began to treat of righteousness, self-control and the coming judgment." With this sentence from the preaching of St. Paul, we have the essence of what he has to say. What does "righteousness" mean? Is it the role of grace, the sinlessness of Jesus and our salvation? I see a need to study this word and see how Paul uses it within his writings. Self-control, self-restraint—these I understand. There is need of putting handlebars on the desires of the flesh. There is a need to say no to self and this can be expressed in many ways.

Judgment. *There is Paul standing before the Roman court being judged, and he sees himself and all humankind standing before You, Father, in that final day of judgment. Only on that last day will we see justice combined with mercy. I will see myself in my nothingness coming forth from Your eternal Love.*

Our great battles are the little struggles within: namely to say no to anger, envy, lust, gluttony—the desires for special foods prepared in special ways—and on and on.

I remember clearly the first intentional sin in my life. Some of the other boys of the neighborhood had taken packages of seeds from the stand outside Morgan's store next door. It was spring and I must have been five or six. I walked past that store and saw the packages of seeds with all the pictures of vegetables on them. I saw a package of corn seeds and since no one was looking, out went my hand, and I walked away with my treasure. What was I going to do with a package of seeds?

There was Hennie, Henry Kinoski, my friend. Hennie gave me my first lesson in farming. The seeds had to be planted in the ground, and then they would grow and produce corn. We went behind the Morgan store, dug a hole, and I suggested that we plant the entire package in that one hole so we would get a large plant of corn. I must have been influenced by the story of "Jack and the Beanstalk." We planted that package of seeds, and here I am seventy years later still waiting for that giant stalk of corn to grow.

Throughout my life, I have reached out for other things not belonging to me and nothing has satisfied. *Only You, Father, can fulfill our desires, for our hearts have been made by You and for You.*

Righteousness is a common term in Protestant theology, but in Catholic circles it is seldom used. The word does not even appear in the index of the new Catholic Catechism. Many Protestants stress faith and belief in Jesus for justification and righteousness. In contrast, Catholics often stress self-control. To bring these two viewpoints into focus is to come one step closer to true ecumenism, and then to the Judgment.

4 : 3 0   A M

(A c t s   2 6)   *Paul speaks before King Agrippa about the hope of a promise made by You, God. You have made a promise of the Resurrection of the dead and Jesus is the first proof of this promise.* Here I am awaiting my own passion, death, and resurrection. I am not sure what all this means. Jesus has risen, but His members have yet to rise from the dead. This is our Holy Saturday.

Paul once again tells his conversion story with a few minor changes in details. He stresses that he is called to preach the forgiveness of sins, faith in Jesus, and that those who are converted by his preaching should act in conformity to their belief.

4 : 3 0   A M

(A c t s   2 6)   King Agrippa accuses Paul of being out of his mind, then a short time later says that Paul will soon persuade him to become a Christian. In reply Paul says, "'I wish before God that not only you but all who have heard me today would come to be as I am—except for these chains.'" What does it mean to be a Christian without chains? What does it mean to be a Christian *with* chains? Chains hinder us from moving about freely. *In some sense sickness is a chain, this body is a chain since it also hinders me from coming to You, Father. Sin hinders the soul from coming to You. Anything, or any person, or any habit of sin that hinders me from coming to You is a chain. Father, set me free that I might come to You without chains.*

4 : 3 0   A M

I n   A c t s   2 7   St. Luke, Paul's traveling companion, gives us a real travelogue of their trip to Rome. Human nature is more inclined to listen to the experts rather than to the saints. Paul could foresee problems. Danger to cargo, to ship, to life, and yet the journey continued.

I am reminded of the travelogues of our Abbot General, Dom Bernardo Olivera, who travels around the world visiting different monasteries. Dom Augustine Roberts, his secretary, has been writing his travelogues and at present his seventh Chronicle letter of the Abbot General's trips is being read to us in the refectory. He has been describing the synaxis that took place at Citeaux in March at which Jacki represented the Lay Cistercians. He then goes on to write of the 900th anniversary of the celebration at Citeaux at which I was privileged to be present.

I recall the visits of the former Abbot General, Dom Ambrose Southerly, and of his secretary, Dom Jacque Briere, to Africa. When they arrived, the quality of the food for the chaplains improved. The General reminded us that, during his visits, the chaplains usually remark, "We don't always eat like this."

The Abbot General also had to decide if Scott, our German shepherd, was fulfilling her obligations to pray the office since she always slept during the time of prayer. At the beginning of each office, Scott would make the rounds in the choir of nuns and sniff out each person. If there was a stranger in choir, she would begin to bark. She would then go before the altar and sleep. *Perhaps she was praying in her own unique way to You.*

After the office, Scott would lead the procession to the refectory walking before the superior, Mother Margaret Mary. There, Scott and Frisky, another dog, would wait to be fed. In the early days of the foundation, the chaplains ate with the nuns and since we were fed meat at times, Scott and Frisky were always at my side.

Once, when Boogy, another German shepherd owned by one of our neighbors, was within our enclosure, Father Andrew came along and wanted to enter the chapel. Not being sure of Boogy, Father Andrew took off his belt and was going to defend himself as he made his way into the chapel. When I saw this, I plunged towards Boogy and held him back as Andrew walked by. I am sure there would have been bloodshed if I had not done this.

4 : 3 0   A M

(A c t s   2 7)   Paul continues on his trip to Rome and the ship runs into a terrible storm. He chides his shipmates by saying they should have listened to him and not continued the trip. He then says, "Last night there was standing beside me an angel of the God to whom I belong and whom I serve, and he said, 'Do not be afraid, Paul. You are destined to appear before Caesar. . . .'" He tells his traveling companions to trust in God, and that they would end up on an island. *Paul sees the future in Your eternal* Now. *Do I trust well enough in You as I walk into the future of Your eternal now? When will I be able to trust You as I should?*

Not only is the future present in You, but also the past. One of our neighbors in Africa was Mr. Williams. Mr. Williams and his twin sister were born in the Abakaliki area of Nigeria where twins were usually killed, because it was believed that one of them was conceived by an evil spirit. An Episcopalian minister rescued Mr. Williams and his twin sister from certain death when they were infants and sent them to the States. Here they were educated. His sister became a dentist, and he went to the University of Tuskegee, Alabama.

After retiring, Mr. Williams decided to return to the Abakaliki area to work among his own people. He established a poultry farm which he later turned into a pig farm. He also had a faith-healing ministry. Since there are always sick people, there were always customers. I am not sure of his mode of healing, but I know that some strange things happened just before his wife's death. A goat died at her feet a few days before she passed away and she seemed to have had a premonition that she was soon to pass over into the next world. *How do we discern, Father, when dreams come from You?*

I am also reminded of the school teacher who once came to me saying he was under a curse because he had turned his back to the juju. It seems that he had gone to hear a voice speaking from a stone in a stream and the voice told him to leave everything and solicit people to come for healing. The voice from the stone would tell people what had to be offered by way of money or goods in order to be healed. In time, the business became so lucrative that the voice moved to a building, and from different places in the floor spoke to people telling them what to do. At once I thought of how someone probably headed to an electronics store to buy equipment and remote control sound systems to set up this business. I did not share this view with the school teacher, but simply prayed over him to be delivered from the curse and, sure enough, he was healed.

4 : 3 0   A M

(A c t s   2 7)   At last, Paul's shipmates listen to him. He tells them of the consequences that will bear if people do not follow his instructions. He speaks of the future as present and then goes on to tell his 276 companions to eat. I cannot help feeling that Paul must have celebrated Eucharist as the few Christians broke bread together. *You,*

*Father, saved them from the storm and also from the soldiers
that wanted to kill all the prisoners. Indeed, You are the Master
of it all.*

This storm from which You delivered Paul reminds me
of the time Dad shared his story of a return trip from Italy
in 1924. My sister, Catherine, brother Anthony, and Uncle
Sam were with him on this return trip from Sicily. A storm
came up and, as Dad said, it was the most fearful storm of
his life. It was so violent, the railings of the ship were
bent. They prayed and invoked the intercession of
Christopher Columbus. Dad not only feared for himself,
but especially for the three children. He attributed their
deliverance to the altar linens he was carrying as a gift to
the church. He was indeed a man of prayer and a man of
faith.

4 : 3 0   A M

(A c t s   2 8)   Unlike Ireland, Malta had its snakes.
Paul had an encounter with a viper. He then began his
ministry of healing. Seemingly this is not a normal part of
the evangelization of Paul. Luke makes sure to record the
healings.

Have I seen people healed through my prayers? Only
yesterday, Julie returned to thank me for the healing of
her arms. Last week, I prayed over her and anointed her
with oil. *It is not the power of my prayers or that of the oil,
but the conjunction of all prayer in unison with Your will,
Father, that brings about healing. Some people I have prayed
over have been healed while others have died. This is part of
Your mystery.*

I remember one minister known for his healing power praying over a woman named Roberta, who had multiple sclerosis. He accused her of lacking the faith to be healed. To have the faith to believe that one will be healed is also Your gift, Father.

When I learned that I had hepatitis B back in 1982, I was convinced that I would be healed the following week. It was shortly after making the foundation for the nuns at Nigeria that I began to feel miserable. I was admitted to the new hospital at Ihala. My weight was dropping a half-pound a day and I could not tolerate food. Even water had a strange taste. Nothing seemed to help. I became convinced that if I remained in that hospital they would eventually carry me out to the morgue. I was the only white man in that place and they tried to prepare food that I might be able to eat. Elbow macaroni was served day after day. Finally I decided to leave while I still had strength enough to walk.

The next day, just as I was planning to run away from the place, to my surprise the doctor came in and said they were dismissing me. My sickness was psychosomatic. A priest gave me a ride to a town called "9 Mile" and from there I took a taxi to within two miles of the monastery of Mount Calvary at Awhum. I did not have the strength to walk the last two miles and sat on the side of the road with tears in my eyes. Along came a man on a motorcycle and gave me the needed lift.

When the superior, Fr. Paul, saw my condition, he decided to drive me to Dr. Anidi, an Ibo trained in Germany. The doctor did the blood work and told me to come back the next day. I was told that I had hepatitis. With a sigh of relief I thanked God that it was not psychosomatic.

Dr. Anidi told me to return, and he would tell me what kind of hepatitis I had. The following day I was told that I had hepatitis B and I should go home, rest, and come back the following week. I told him, "I'll be back next week, and you will dismiss me." I left his office and prayed to Sister Justina who had died of hepatitis in a hospital ward in England the preceding year. I said, "Sister Justina, it is your fault that I am here. You invited me to be your chaplain. Here I am and I have the same sickness from which you died. Please get me cured!"

The following week I returned to Dr. Anidi. He said my blood was almost clear and to come back in two days. When I returned at the end of the week, he said my blood was clear. My reply was, "Doctor didn't I tell you I would be back this week and you would dismiss me?" He said, "Yes." Then I told him that I had prayed to Sister Justina. The doctor looked at me over the top of his glasses, tapped his pen on the desk, and said, "Let me tell you something. Six out of ten people die from this in Nigeria and it takes six months to a year for the rest to recover." *Thank You, Father, for healing.*

4 : 3 0   A M

(A c t s   2 8)   It seems like we have traveled with Paul for a long time and at last we have made it to Rome with all expenses paid by the government. What influence did Paul have upon the guards who stayed with him? *Did any of them come to have faith in Your Son, Jesus?*

It is my conviction that Paul lived at the present site of the Church of St. Stephen Rotunda not far from the Roman Coliseum. Archeologists have discovered the barracks of Roman soldiers there. It seems that the early Christians of Rome would have built a church on the site where Paul evangelized for two years. It was Stephen who prayed for his enemy Saul, and it is here in the heart of the Roman Empire that Paul was bringing the world to Jesus.

At Tre Fontani, the traditional site of Paul's beheading, I asked for Paul's intercession before going on into Nigeria to work with the monks of Mt. Calvary Monastery at Awhum.

I ask Paul to bless these writings about him, now being scribbled in the shade of this night in this Abbey church. *Bless all those who may read these lines, and may they go out to proclaim to the ends of the earth their love for Your Son, Jesus.*

4 : 3 0   A M

(A c t s   2 8)   Luke ends his account by telling us how Paul lived rather than how he died. We behold Paul with the Scriptures before him surrounded by fellow Jews arguing all day long ". . . and trying to persuade them about Jesus." Who is Jesus? Paul tries to prove that Jesus is the Messiah. It is Jesus, not Paul or Saul, or Luke, or me. It is Jesus, Jesus, Jesus! Luke tells us very little of what Paul taught other than he taught about Jesus. To know what Paul taught we must instead search out his letters. There, we do not behold a Jesus that performs miracles, or Jesus the storyteller, but the Jesus living in His members. Jesus is living in you and in me.

Here we each sit alone—I in the Abbey church and you wherever you are as you read these words, encountering God in the shade of day or night—pondering the closing words of the book of Acts.

Father, I come before You praying in the shade of this night knowing that the totality of human history stands present before You. Past, present, and future are all in Your eternal *Now*. Before You we bring this book to a close knowing that it is Your light that illuminates all.

Afterword

IN OTHER WORDS:
AN INTRODUCTION TO
CONTEMPLATIVE PRAYER

To pray implies that there is someone who hears, who listens, who understands. Prayer is common to all cultures. While in Africa, I beheld the pagans, the animists, who built small shrines of bamboo and grass to pay honor to "the power" who gave life to water gushing from the side of a hill, or gave life to a giant tree. There they slaughtered their sacrifice of chickens or poured out palm wine or even Coca-Cola. The Native Americans who once occupied our monastery property also had their rituals to the invisible world.

We are especially indebted to the Jewish people who have taught us to turn to a personal God who made all and knows all, even future events. The Psalms, prayers inherited from the synagogue, are gold mines of prayer.

In Africa, I often heard Muslims crying out over loud-speakers to make sure their prayers were heard before the coming of the dawn. I saw truck drivers pull to the side of the road at the closing of the day, pull out their prayer rugs, and prostrate themselves toward Mecca. Once, while traveling with a Dominican priest in Northern Nigeria— Muslim country—we also pulled to the side of the road, pulled out our prayer rugs, and said vespers together.

I am reminded of my visit to Nigeria in 1995. I had arranged to fly out of the Atlanta airport and meet Dom John Eudes, Abbot of Genesee Abbey, in Amsterdam and from there we would fly together into Lagos. While waiting in line at Amsterdam to get flight information about his arrival time, I saw a nun in the line next to me. She introduced herself as Sister Paula, a member of our daughter house in Venezuela. She was returning from Indonesia. Indeed, the world is small. When Dom John Eudes arrived in Amsterdam, we proceeded to the chapel located on the second floor of the airport. While we were celebrating Mass, a Muslim walked in, got out his prayer rug, and made his prostrations towards Mecca. Then a white Protestant minister, followed by a black minister, came in to pray in the back of the small chapel. Here we were, from around the world, gathered in this small chapel, praying to our God: Muslim, Protestant, and

Catholic. Afterwards I commented about this to Sister Paula who, in turn, reminded me that she had with her a relic of Blessed Gabriella, a Cistercian nun who gave her life for unity.

Libraries are filled with books on methods and techniques of prayer. I write as a monk who has struggled with prayer. Over fifty years of praying the Liturgy of the Hours composed of the Psalms and other Scripture readings have helped me to arrive at my own method.

As a young monk, I found the early hours of prayer my battlefield with sleep. After World War II there was a shortage of choir books due to the influx of vocations. Instead of having a giant-sized Psalter in front of us, we novices were given a small Latin book called a breviary, made up of the Psalms and other prayers. I can still remember during vigils, about 2:45 AM, when the breviary fell from my hands for the first time, and made a crashing sound as it hit the floor and woke me up. I had to prostrate myself before the community with my face to the floor, waiting until the superior gave me a signal to return to my place in choir. After this happened a second time, I decided to do something about it. I began searching for a piece of string. When I found a piece, I tied one end to the breviary and the other end to my wrist. The next time the breviary fell from my hands, it stopped in mid-air and woke me up. Indeed, those early hours became my battlefield with sleep.

No longer do we monks arise at 2 AM on weekdays, 1:30 AM on Sundays, and 1 AM on feast days. Here at Conyers we now arise at 3:45 AM. Vigils begins at 4 AM. Thus begins the daily round of community prayer. The cycle of psalms that we pray each day is spread over a two-week period and interspersed with other Scripture readings from the two Testaments and from readings of the Fathers of the church.

Now I look upon those early hours as the most sacred portion of the monastic day. Vigils, the first prayer service of the day, consists of a hymn, three psalms, and usually a reading from the Old Testament. Then follows a half-hour of silent prayer. During this time, I often go to the corner near the entry to the Guesthouse and begin pondering the Old Testament reading to see where this takes me. My reflections often lead me into silence in the presence of the Father. I have written about these experiences of prayer in this book.

Now you know the essence of my method of prayer. Some would call it a type of *lectio*— pondering on the text. Others would say it is a type of Centering Prayer, although I feel free to depart from some techniques taught with that way of praying. I desire, as much as possible, to give freedom for the Holy Spirit to act within me and lead me wherever He might want to take me.

I believe, as the Church teaches, that the Liturgy of the Hours is the prayer of Jesus as He continues to pray within His Church today. This prayer of Jesus among His people is the daily prayer of the monk. The Psalms vocalize this prayer which expresses so clearly the depth of human emotion.

Since the terrorist attacks of September 11, 2001, I have taken note of how often the Psalms speak of enemies, adversaries, or foes. What was once an abstract concept has now become a sad reality. I find myself praying to God for justice, but also for mercy.

To Christians, Jesus becomes the model for prayer since we believe Him to be the Eternal Son of the invisible God who made all. In the Gospel of Matthew Jesus gives us teachings on prayer. There He says, "'When you pray, go to your private room, and when you have shut the door, pray to your Father who is in that secret place.'" According to the original Greek this "inner room" or "secret place" implies a storeroom. In the Greek, He not only tells us to close the door, but to lock it. This storeroom, or cellar, is the place where one might store up provisions for a time of need. You, dear reader, have spent some time in that cellar earlier in this book. That cellar is the very center of our being. We encounter God there.

When we pray, we believe that there is someone who is able to listen to prayer, someone to whom we may turn with all our concerns. This creates questions. Which way do we turn to find that someone to whom prayer is directed? Is that someone out there, or if not, where? The teaching of Vatican II as found in the document *The Church in the Modern World* tells us that the direction to go is within:

> Deep within his conscience man discovers a law which he has not laid upon himself but which he must obey. Its voice, ever calling him to love and to do what is good and to avoid evil, tells him inwardly at the right moment to do this, shun that. For man has in his heart a law inscribed by God. His dignity lies in observing this law, and by it, he will be judged. There he is alone with God whose voice echoes in his depths. (#16)

At the very center of our being we discover we are alone with God. This is the heart of all prayer, the place where a silent dialogue without words begins, even within a child. Pope John Paul II, when speaking to about a million youth from all over the world gathered in Denver in 1993, said:

> Do not stifle your conscience! Conscience is the most secret core of the sanctuary of a person where he is alone with God.

This core of our being is also our conscience, the place where we learn to communicate with the One who hears all prayer. All prayer ultimately comes to this sacred space. On December 23, 1941, Thomas Merton in one of his earliest entries in his journal, as a novice at Gethsemani Abbey, wrote of this sacred space:

> In the middle of myself, so to speak, (because it is really in no place at all, but in the infinity of the spirit) there is an emptiness without any features at all, without stars or light or any wind, without movement, without walls. It is an emptiness full of silence, sometimes cool and sometimes sweet and sometimes frightening. There with the grace of God, I retire and walk, wondering "Where is Jesus? He is here, somewhere: not in the other parts of my mind, but really here. But where?" (Taken from *The Merton Seasonal*, Winter 2000.)

I have often read this quote to people and asked them to imagine themselves walking in that special place, that is no place; that has neither stars nor light nor wind nor movement nor walls. In that empty space full of silence, for some a frightful place to be, one slowly becomes aware of a Presence. The experience of this Presence often cannot be put into words.

In Africa, the monks at Awhum referred to this inward journey as the "Prayer of the Heart." Our brothers and sisters from the Orthodox Churches also refer to prayer in this way. Someone recently told me that Blessed John XXIII, the pope who inspired the Second Vatican Council, when praying would imagine himself going under water, resting in silence. Catherine de Hueck Doherty also writes in her book, *Molchanie*, of entering into the sea of God's silence. Pope Pius XII on February 2, 1941, said:

> To seek our God, to find Him, it is enough to enter into yourselves, morning, night, or at any moment of the day. If you are joyfully in the state of grace, you will see in the intimacy of your soul with the eyes of faith God ever present as an immensely kind Father, ready to hear your requests and tell you also what He expects of you.

Earlier in this book, I referred to this sacred place as a cellar. As I slowly became comfortable with entering this cellar, I in fact entered into the very center of my being, there to be alone with the Father. That sacred space is also the Heart of Jesus. It was Julian of Norwich who saw:

> With a smile and rejoicing our Lord looked into His wounded side, and there He showed me this beautiful place large enough for all of mankind who shall be saved to rest there in peace and love.

For some, especially those outside of the Catholic tradition, the special devotion to the Heart of Jesus may be hard to understand. A nurse friend of mine shared with me that her Protestant co-worker commented that she found pictures of Jesus with His heart exposed and burning with flame offensive. Sally responded, "You like to imagine yourself inviting Jesus into your heart, but we Catholics like to imagine ourselves entering the Heart of Jesus." Once I shared this story with a group of retreatants in our guesthouse, and a Presbyterian minister commented, "Indeed, every Sunday, I ask my congregation to invite Jesus into their hearts. I've never thought of asking them to consider entering into the Heart of Jesus."

In order for the Lord to manifest His being in the center of *our* being, there may be a need for some housecleaning. At times our awareness of the presence of God is hidden beneath a lifetime of bad memories. There is a need to take these memories to the Father and to silently rest in His presence and wait for His healing. With the surfacing of suppressed childhood fears, there comes forth a sense of freedom as the God-within manifests Himself as merciful and understanding. For some, the recall of suppressed fears of childhood brings up memories of physical, emotional, sexual, or psychological abuse. It is important to remember that the unfolding of childhood trauma may also at times lead one to call on professional help.

Sometimes it is easier to forget rather than recall the reality of life. Some people simply cannot recall the events of the past, while others live in the past and fail to face the reality of the present. I recall a religious woman sharing with me that a close friend, who was in the novitiate with her, was martyred in Central America. Her remains were returned to the States for the funeral. I asked, "Did they have an open casket?" She looked shocked at my question and replied, "I do not remember." After some hesitation she said, "Yes, there was an open casket, but I did not want to remember her as I saw her in the casket."

Indeed, there are times when it is easier to forget than remember. Once the hidden memories of the past begin to surface, there may be a need for someone from the outside to help sort them out. At times such memories may elicit the need of forgiving those involved in bringing about the fears of the past. For some, childhood memories may be memories of joy, while it is the teenage years that are filled with emotional turmoil. God knows the secrets of the heart and to Him we go to expose our wounds, asking for healing for ourselves and for others.

We might consider such thoughts as distractions, but in fact, they are indeed special graces of enlightenment.

Recalling past sins can almost literally haunt us, even after such sins have been confessed. I call this the "purgation of the memories." St. Benedict calls this process "compunction," which, as I mentioned above, means to tear apart the heart through strenuous repentance. Receiving an insight into the potential of evil that dwells within the human heart is humiliating. At these times it is especially important to persist in prayer. Eventually, with God's assistance, we may sense God's forgiveness followed by a deep peace.

So, what is contemplative prayer? St. Teresa of Avila answers: "Contemplative prayer, in my opinion, is nothing else than a close sharing between friends, it means taking time frequently to be alone with Him who we know loves us. . . . Contemplation is the gaze of faith, fixed on Jesus."

A social worker phoned me many years ago wanting to bring some small children from inner-city Atlanta to visit the monastery. The children came. On the lawn just outside the guesthouse was a pile of manure. These children had never seen manure before nor had they ever experienced the smell of it. One of them ran up and said, "What is that?" I blushed, trying to figure out how to describe horse manure. I turned to the social worker and said, "You tell her." She told the child: "This is what you put around the plants to make them grow." She was telling the child where the manure was going, and I was trying to figure out how to tell the child from where it had come. I was looking at it from the wrong end. The recall of past sins can be much like that manure, a simple stimulus for spiritual growth.

Someone once said that contemplative prayer should be as natural as a fish swimming in water, but I think that some people rush into contemplative prayer before they are ready. The process of praying in the cellar is intended to ease one in slowly.

Contemplative prayer depends on God's grace. I am convinced that one is ready to enter into this silent mode of listening and awareness only when the inner turmoil of distractions quiets down. For some this will take time.

St. Bernard holds that the first step to knowing God is to know oneself. In order to really know yourself, you must first understand from whence you have come. As mentioned above, sometimes this will involve doing some house-cleaning in your life and through your memories. Then it will be time to forget. Isaiah expresses this best:

> Forget the former things; do not dwell on the past. See, I am doing a new thing! Now it springs up; do you not perceive it? I am making a way in the desert and streams in the wasteland. . . . Yet you have not

called upon me, O Jacob, you have not wearied yourselves for me, O Israel. . . . But you have burdened me with your sins, and wearied me with your offenses. I, even I, am he who blots out your transgressions, for my own sake, and remembers your sins no more.

If God is able to forget our sins, then there is also a need for us to forget them. The past is past and cannot be relived, but with God's grace something can be done about the present and the future. A septic tank will not work if one keeps stirring up the contents. Let things settle and then the bacteria will do the rest. In the same way there is a need to confess our sins and then simply to trust in God's mercy and stop replaying and reliving the past.

When we first enter into silent prayer, we are often bombarded with distractions. Rather than ignore them or shake them away, I simply tell people to turn their distractions into a prayer and see where things go. I have often been asked to elaborate on how to turn distractions into prayer. Many examples of this are to be found in this book. Simply place them before the Father and ask Him for enlightenment. Each individual will have to work out the details with the help of the Holy Spirit, but after a period of time, the distractions slow down and a blessed monotony sets in. Then one is ready to enter into contemplative prayer and is able to simply sit in God's presence and wait with love.

In Psalm 44 we pray, "he knows the secrets of the heart." If God knows the very secrets of our hearts, then He must be there in the very midst of our being. On that last day, when we exit this mortal body, I believe one of our greatest surprises will be the discovery that God was so near to us, in fact within us, and we did not recognize Him.

Prayer is a unique experience for each person. In prayer we encounter the God who has been waiting since the very first moment of our existence. Together in this book we have encountered God in the cellar, yes, even in the darkest part of the cellar, the banana room; in the light; and finally in the shade. Yes, to that sacred place in the midst of our conscience, within our so-called cellar, we return to be alone with the God who knows us and loves us. May the God of merciful love bless you.

Appendix

G R O U P   D I S C U S S I O N   G U I D E

The following series of questions are presented to facilitate discussions about the contents of this book.

Chapter 1

1. What was your first reaction on entering into your cellar?
2. What were some of your fears that surfaced in your cellar?
3. How did you process these fears?

4. What are your first memories concerning your father, mother, brothers, sisters, grandparents, and others?
5. What were the outstanding things they taught you?
6. What was your first experience with death?
7. How did you handle it?
8. Are you willing to share your fears with others?
9. Does your family still retain some ethnic customs? Ethnic foods?
10. Did you have any experiences of God as a child?
11. Do you like to cook?
12. In what ways is cooking similar to prayer in your life?
13. Are you able to pray as you cook?
14. Are you able to make your cooking a prayer?

Chapter 2

1. Are you afraid of darkness?
2. Do you need a night-light?
3. Were you afraid as a child?
4. How did others help you handle those fears?
5. What were your first impressions or experiences of love?
6. What are the cellars in your life?
7. Whose love and acceptance did you crave as a child?
8. What does love mean to you now?
9. Can you recall your first sins?
10. How did God speak to you through your conscience?
11. How did you respond to the voice of conscience?
12. What were your first impressions of sexuality?
13. Were you afraid to talk about them with others?
14. Can you recall your experiences of love as a teenager?
15. How did you handle rejection?
16. What other questions came to mind as you read this chapter?

Chapter 3

1. What experiences in your life were like turning on the lights?
2. Do you believe that dreams speak to you?
3. What books have you read about dreams?
4. Consider making a study of dreams in the Bible.
5. Do you ever write your dreams down?
6. What does it feel like to stand in God's light?
7. Have you ever felt that way?
8. Do you feel that way now?
9. What other questions came to mind as you read this chapter?

Chapter 4

1. How do you react when your spiritual vitality seems to have vanished and you have to face the realities of life?
2. How do you pray when even the Scriptures do not elicit memories in your life?
3. How does silence enter into your prayer?
4. What is the best time of day for you to pray?
5. How do you react when God does not seem to be listening?
6. What is contemplative prayer to you?
7. How have you learned from your sinful mistakes?
8. What mistakes have you made in your life that you would now like to help others to avoid?
9. How do you react to the thought of your own death?
10. Do you fear death?
11. What is the difference between feelings and faith?
12. Should feelings be suppressed?

Afterword

1. How do you make prayer a personal experience?
2. How do you turn distractions into a prayer?
3. How can you make your enemies your friends?
4. Are there sins in your life you have never confronted or confessed? (fifth step of AA)
5. Are there sins for which you have not forgiven yourself—or others?
6. What is the "manure" in your life that God used to make you grow? How did it happen?

Notes

Introduction

p. xvii   "'But when you pray, . . . '" Matthew 6:6

p. xviii "'Unless you change . . . '" Matthew 18:3

Chapter One

p. 10   " . . . I thought of the olden days, . . ." Psalm 77:5-6

p. 10   "If I climb the heavens, . . ." Psalm 139:8

p. 17   "our almsgiving must be . . ." Matthew 6:3

p. 24   "the scraps remaining, . . ." Matthew 14:20

p. 26   "I live now . . ." Galatians 2:20

p. 29   "Peace I bequeath to you, . . ." John 14:27

Chapter Two

p. 38   Jesus tells us in Matthew . . . Matthew 6:6

p. 44   St. Paul suggested to the Corinthians
        1 Corinthians 11:17–31

p. 47   "' . . . give light to those who live in darkness. . . .'"
          Luke 1:79a

p. 52   "Where could I go to escape. . . ?" Psalm 139:7-8

Chapter Three

p. 68   "'Then you will remember . . .'" Ezekiel 36:31

p. 71   "'There are two nations . . .'" Genesis 25:23a

p. 71   . . . Jacob's dream in Genesis. Genesis 28:10–19

p. 72   "To win Rachel . . ." Genesis 29:20

p. 73   " . . . greatly afraid and distressed. . ." Genesis 32:7

p. 73   "'I came into your presence . . .'" Genesis 33:10

p. 74   . . . revealed of you in Genesis
         Genesis 35:14-15

p. 75   "Joseph was seventeen years old . . ."
         Genesis 37:2

p. 75   "I AM who I AM." Exodus 3:14a

p. 76   "'I am your brother Joseph'" see Genesis 45:3a

p. 76   "We together are Christ's body."
         1 Corinthians 12:27a

p. 76   "'This is my commandment: . . .'" John 15:12

p. 77   "He satisfies my desires. . . ." paraphrased from
         Psalm 103:5, 7-8, 9, 10, 13-14 NIV

p. 77   In Exodus 4 You spoke . . see Exodus 4:1–8

p. 77   "Speak, Yahweh, for your servant is hearing. . . ."
         1 Samuel 3:10 NIV

p. 78   "At various times in the past . . ." Hebrews 1:12

p. 79   "'Stand firm . . .'" Exodus 14:13-14

p. 79   "'Be still, and know that I am God.'"
         Psalm 46:10a NIV

p. 86   "'It was the same Moses . . .'" Acts 7:35

p. 87   " . . . gazed into heaven . . .'" Acts 7:55

p. 89   "'Now, Peter, kill and eat!'" Acts 10:13

p. 90   Peter tell . . . Cornelius Acts 10:28

p. 96   "'Your sons and daughters . . .'"
         Joel 2:28, Acts 2:17

Chapter Four

p. 102   "I am the light of the world." John 8:12

p. 106   "' . . . not to preach the word in Asia." Acts 16:6

p. 107   "Late that night Paul and Silas . . ." Acts 16:25

p. 108   "'[God] is not far from any of us, . . .'"
         Acts 17:28

p. 109 "'Do not be afraid to speak out, . . .'" Acts 18:9-10

p. 110 "God is light; . . ." 1 John 1:5b–7

p. 110 "Send out your light and your truth; . . ."
Psalm 43:3

p. 110 "'I, the light, have come . . .'" John 12:46

p. 112 "'Great is Diana of the Ephesians!'"
Acts 19:28b

p. 113 " . . . a lamp to my feet, . . ."
Psalm 119:105

p. 113 "Eutychus who was sitting on . . ." Acts 20:9

p. 117 "He fell to the ground, . . ." Acts 9:4

p. 117 "'You utter fraud, you impostor, . . .'"
Acts 13:10-11

p. 120 "'Courage! You have borne witness . . .'"
Acts 23:11

p. 121 "'I . . . do my best to keep . . .'"
Acts 24:16

p. 122 "He began to treat of righteousness, . . ."
Acts 24:25

p. 124 "'I wish before God . . .'" Acts 26:29

p. 126 "'Last night I was standing . . .'" Acts 27:24

p. 128 Paul had an encounter with a viper Acts 28:1–6

p. 131 " . . . and trying to persuade them . . ."
Acts 28:23

Afterword

p. 137 "'When you pray . . .'" Matthew 6:6

p. 142 "Forget the former things . . ."
Isaiah 43:18-19, 22, 24-25 NIV

p. 143 "he knows the secrets of the heart."
Psalm 44:21b NIV

About Paraclete Press

Who We Are

Paraclete Press is an ecumenical publisher of books on Christian spirituality for people of all denominations and backgrounds.

We publish books that represent the wide spectrum of Christian belief and practice—from Catholic to Evangelical to liturgical to Orthodox.

We market our books primarily through booksellers; we are what is called a "trade" publisher, which means that we like it best when readers buy our books from booksellers, our partners in successfully reaching as wide of an audience as possible.

We are uniquely positioned in the marketplace without connection to a large corporation or conglomerate and with informal relationships to many branches and denominations of faith, rather than a formal relationship to any single one. We focus on publishing a diversity of thoughts and perspectives—the fruit of our diversity as a company.

What We Are Doing

Paraclete Press is publishing books that show the diversity and depth of what it means to be Christian. We publish books that reflect the Christian experience across many cultures, time periods, and houses of worship.

We publish books about spiritual practice, history, ideas, customs, and rituals, and books that nourish the vibrant life of the church.

We have several different series of books within Paraclete Press, including the bestselling Living Library series of modernized classic texts, A Voice from the Monastery—giving voice to men and women monastics on what it means to live a spiritual life today, and Many Mansions—for exploring the riches of the world's religious traditions and discovering how other faiths inform Christian thought and practice.

Learn more about us at our website:
www.paracletepress.com, or call us toll-free at
800- 451-5006.

Other books in the A Voice from the Monastery Series:

Seeking His Mind
40 Meetings with Christ
M. Basil Pennington, O.C.S.O.
176 pages
ISBN: 1-55725-308-0
$14.95 Hardcover

If Hindus have Yoga and Buddhists have meditation, what is the Christian method of transformation? Fr. Pennington's answer is *lectio divina*—hearing and meditating on the word of God. In this spirit, he offers forty meditations on scriptural texts of the life and words of Christ, providing an ideal resource to start or expand *lectio divina* practice.

A Selection of the Catholic Book Club

"Easy, beautiful writing style . . . perfect for daily Lenten devotions, but could be used at any time of year."—*Publishers Weekly*

"Cistercian Father Basil Pennington has a distinguished history of teaching and practicing Centering Prayer. This book is the fruit of that long engagement. Like the good householder of the Gospel, his reflections teach us how to bring forth old things and new."
—Lawrence S. Cunningham,
John A. Obrien Professor of Theology, The University of Notre Dame

The Place We Call Home
Spiritual Pilgrimage as a Path to God
Murray Bodo, O.F.M.
116 pages
ISBN: 1-55725-357-9
$14.95 Paperback

With over twenty-five years of experience in making and leading spiritual pilgrimages, Fr. Murray Bodo is an open-hearted guide to this ancient tradition. He leads us to traditional pilgrim sites such as Rome and Assisi, and also on journeys of memory—back to our childhood, and to the churches and landscapes of our past. Ultimately, we find that spiritual pilgrimage not only enriches our lives, but transforms us into the people that we are called to become.

"Now you can wander and wonder with a true spiritual guide!
Fr. Murray, like a good novel, will offer your pilgrimage a good
beginning, an inspiring middle, and an even better end."
Fr. Richard Rohr, O.F.M.
Author of *Everything Belongs: The Gift of Contemplative Prayer*

Available from most booksellers or through Paraclete Press:
www.paracletepress.com; 1-800-451-5006.
Try your local bookstore first.